# SWARTHMORE'S CENTURY
# A LEEDS EXPERIMENT IN ADULT
# EDUCATION 1909–2009

**by Tom Steele**

First published in Great Britain 2009

Published by Swarthmore Education Centre
2-7 Woodhouse Square
Leeds LS3 1AD
Tel: 0113 243 2210
e-mail: info@swarthmore.org.uk
www.swarthmore.org.uk

Swarthmore is a company limited by guarantee.
Registered in England and Wales No.4527579
Registered Charity No.1094451

ISBN 978-0-9562800-0-8

Designed by dg3 design. www.dg3.co.uk

Printed by Beamreach Printing

Copyright © Swarthmore Education Centre/Tom Steele 2009

Swarthmore Education Centre and Tom Steele assert the moral right to be identified as the authors of this work.

All rights reserved. No part of this publication may be reproduced, stored in a retrieval system, or transmitted, in any form or by any means, electronic, mechanical, photocopying, recording or otherwise, without prior written permission of Swarthmore Education Centre.

This book is sold subject to the condition that is shall not by way of trade or otherwise be lent, re-sold, hired our or otherwise circulated without the publisher's prior consent in any form of binding or cover other than that in which it is published and without a similar condition including this condition being imposed on the subsequent purchaser.

# Contents

| | | |
|---|---|---|
| **Acknowledgements** | | 4 |
| **Foreword** | | 5 |
| **Chapter 1** | Introduction, Leeds and the Quaker Renaissance | 6 |
| **Chapter 2** | 'A Place for Friends', 1909–1920 | 20 |
| **Chapter 3** | Social Justice and International Understanding, 1920–1939 | 40 |
| **Chapter 4** | War, Reconstruction and Revival, 1939–1960 | 56 |
| **Chapter 5** | The Making of a Radical Arts Centre, 1960–1973 | 78 |
| **Chapter 6** | Social Purpose, Community Action and the Arts, 1973–1993 | 98 |
| **Chapter 7** | Educational Partnerships, Targets and Contracts, 1993–2009 | 120 |
| **Appendices** | 1 Wardens and Directors | 140 |
| | 2 Annual Income | 141 |
| **References** | | 142 |

## Acknowledgements

This is not the last word on Swarthmore, which moves confidently into its second century and has every reason to see a third. As a very bold experiment in adult education it has frequently attracted comment, from the *1919 Report* to Alan Tuckett of NIACE, and several short histories have already been written at various points in its career. As befits the occasion, this is very much a celebratory history and one that is unavoidably coloured by my own experience of working there as a WEA Tutor Organiser from 1975 to 1988, an exhilarating time. However, once Swarthmore's papers have been lodged with the Brotherton Library at Leeds University, they should be available for proper scholarly research.

I should very much like to thank all those who have helped me write this. Malcolm Walters very kindly offered me the opportunity at Jill Liddington's suggestion and heroically dragged old cardboard boxes of dusty log-books, newspaper cuttings, photos, annual reports and sessional programmes down from the attic. I think all living Wardens and Directors past and present have commented on chapter drafts and added further insights. These include Brian Thompson, Martin Russell, Guy Farrar, Ann Walker and Maggi Butterworth. I'm very grateful to Freda Matthews, Gay Bennett, Marjorie Hall, John Arnison and Kay Stainsby for their reflections on chapter drafts and for other personal information. Gay's and Marjorie's notes for a history in 1999 have been especially useful. The undergraduate thesis on Swarthmore by my former colleague at Leeds University, Janet Coles, has also been very helpful. Special thanks are due to Janet Douglas of Leeds Metropolitan University for putting me right on Leeds history (and punctuation) and further insights into the Harvey family. My colleague Mark Freeman in the Department of Economic and Social History at Glasgow University has very generously shared his understanding of the Quaker Renaissance in Yorkshire and his books *The Joseph Rowntree Charitable Trust, A Study in Quaker Philanthropy and Adult Education 1904-1954* (2004) and *Quaker Extension c.1905–1930: The Yorkshire 1905 Committee* (2008) are essential reading for anyone who wants to follow this history up. Many thanks to Lynne Gostick for proof-reading and, as always, helpful suggestions, to Patrick Hall for final proofing and to Richard Honey for his editing, sourcing and presentation of images and wonderfully elegant production.

Tom Steele, June 2009

# Foreword

Swarthmore wears its distinctions very lightly and this book is a real eye-opener into the sheer amount of faith, hope and charity – in the original and best sense of charity, meaning kindness – which has gone into the centre over its hundred years. It is hard to think of a better example of George Fox's famous injunction to Quakers to walk cheerfully over the world, seeking that of God in others and doing everything they can to encourage it.

I don't think that Quakers will be upset if we take 'God' to mean goodness, because Tom Steele's history consists of 80 pages which tell a story of consistently good work. Given the popularity of what cynics call 'misery memoirs', you may wonder if this is a recipe for success, but you need have no fear. I started reading Page 1 at teatime and finished Page 81 before the News at Ten.

There are characters aplenty such as an MI5 spy – or was he? Curious episodes include the affair of the stolen skeleton, which may have influenced the lucrative career of that Leeds lad, Damien Hirst. Given the constant need to watch the money, I was also pleased to read that Libya owes us £3,000 in unpaid student fees, backdated to 1984. Now that the British and Libyan governments seem to be friends again, perhaps we could send a reminder bill.

Everyone who has studied at Swarthmore holds the place and its people in great affection, even those who failed to make progress, such as myself. My only physical memento of classes is an atrocious oil painting of a ploughed field beside the ring road in Adel. In spite of the best efforts of my tutor, I could never remember whether you painted dark colours on first or light ones, and the result was mud. The field consisted of mud, but my mud didn't even look like mud. But as you will easily imagine, everyone was very kind.

In one of the most famous introductions to a great work of fiction, Tolstoy began Anna Karenina by asserting that "All happy families are alike; every unhappy family is unhappy in its own way." He was wrong. Swarthmore has always been a happy family of a particularly unusual and fascinating kind, and Tom deserves our warmest thanks for showing how and why this has been and remains the case. Now for the next hundred years!

by **Martin Wainwright**
President of Swarthmore Council and Northern Editor of the Guardian newspaper

**CHAPTER 1**

# Introduction: Leeds and the Quaker Renaissance

*When Swarthmore was started there were few opportunities for wider education for the majority of citizens. The University Extension Movement had done good service, but did not touch the lives of the mass of the workers. The WEA had but recently entered upon its great work, the local authority's task in adult education was confined to commercial and technical courses. The Adult School movement was endeavouring to widen its scope in various ways, but lacked the means to provide systematic study in its atmosphere of friendship. For the first time this became possible for many who came to the educational settlement, finding there a home in which mind and spirit might widen and deepen.*
(Edmund Harvey, 1949: 1)

## A Tale of Two Cities

Maybe Leeds was always a boom town. Its population had trebled in the eighteenth century to 30,000 as a result of the production of woollen cloths and the medieval market town centred on Briggate and the Leeds Bridge began to show something of what it was to become, a great manufacturing and commercial town. Then under the pressure of the Industrial Revolution in the first half of the nineteenth century, its population swelled again by no less than five times to 150,000. Leeds now harvested a wide diversity of products from coal and chemicals, tool and machine making to leather and pottery and fielded a range of processes for clothing manufacture. By the end of the century commerce flourished and to its industrial base added banking, 'friendly' building societies and insurance companies, which transformed it once again. Great public institutions were built, such as Broderick's Town Hall, Corn Exchange and Leeds Institute, while a nymph-adorned City Square, a fine public library, art gallery and green parks in Roundhay, Meanwood and Woodhouse gave it civic dignity. In its many squares, monuments to the bewhiskered founding fathers frowned on passers by, reminding them of the serious business of life. Leeds finally celebrated its prestigious arrival as a chartered city in 1893 and, with the founding of the Yorkshire College for Science which became part of the Victoria University and then the basis of the University of Leeds in 1904, it began to look like a learned place.

With the new wealth came shopping and Leeds became a kind of 'shoppocracy' with shimmering arcades around Briggate, whole shopping streets aglow with gas and in Boar Lane's case electric lighting, as in Atkinson Grimshaw's paintings, and mellow brick and Burmantoft's faience facades around the well-named Commercial Street. Down in the old Leeds market by Vicar's Croft amongst the fruit and veg, Messrs Marks and Spencer had set up their stall. A scene of industry and prosperity if ever there was one, especially if you had the money and leisure to enjoy it.

But industrial boom towns always have their grimmer sides and Leeds was no exception. Beyond the gas-lit glitter of the city centre and the fine Georgian Squares to the east lay the congested courts of poorly-built tenements that ware-housed cheap immigrant labour. The area around the Bank, between the York Road and the river, was one of the mostly densely-packed areas in Europe hosting the Irish labourers who had come to build the canal and the railways, country boys looking for work, political refugees from Europe, hucksters, hustlers and, from the City Fathers' perspective, an unseemly congregation of unwonted malcontents. Closer to town, across the York Road in the 'Leylands' another poor area began, after the twentieth century had turned, to house the thousands of Jews fleeing the Czarist pogroms of Eastern Europe. Mostly composed of craftsmen, fine tradesmen and workers in leather and cloth, this population became the basis for the rapid expansion of clothing and shoe manufacturers that threw up Burtons and other large producers. They didn't always get on well with their neighbours on the other side of the road and skirmishing was frequent. They set up the first clothing workers trade unions too and sheltered many an exile on the run. South of the river Hunslet and Holbeck, later documented in the work of Richard Hoggart, mingled satanic mills and blackened slag heaps with the pinched back-to-backs and reeking middens for which Leeds became infamous.

Muck begot plenty of brass of course and the secret of Leeds's success lay in part in its communications with north and south and east and west as a kind of junction town centrally placed in northern England. Canals, railways and roads now linked it to almost every part of the country and its ports and to the north just about as fine an agricultural scene as you could want. Improved transport also meant a new class of person was also coming to Leeds, attracted by white collar opportunities for supervisors, technicians, teachers, and the kind of lower professional needed for a thriving commercial city. A typical example of one of these, in 1893, was Alfred Orage, a probationary schoolteacher from East Anglia with a missionary zeal. He didn't much like what he saw on his walk down from Chapel Allerton, where he lived, to Ellerby School on the Bank, where he worked, writing: 'down there, the infernal pot is boiling, and steam hangs like a nightmare over the city...thousands of chimneys are allowed to belch their poisonous breaths to be inhaled by human lungs below'. If Leeds was a great toxic beast consuming its workers, the river was not exactly the Jordan either, but an 'oily flowing mud stream, into whose waters no fish may dare enter, on whose banks no leaves can breathe, no trees may grow' (quoted in Steele, 1990: 26). Having tried (and apparently failed) to 'reduce Leeds to Nietzscheanism' through the Arts Club he founded, Orage went on to become a path-breaking journal editor in London. Another associate who went on to greater things was Herbert Read. Though later to become internationally famous as a Modern Art critic, especially through his promotion of surrealism and the work of Henry Moore, Read was at this time a humble bank clerk. Describing his walk through town from Woodhouse Moor, he recorded the scene:

> *I passed through areas in which factories were only relieved by slums, slums by factories – a wilderness of stone and brick, with soot falling like black snow. Drab and stunted wage-slaves drifted through the stink and clatter; tram cars moaned and screeched along their glistening rails, spluttering blue electric sparks. These same wage slaves brought their savings to the bank...greasy coins which blackened the fingers that counted them, and were then entered into pass book permeated by grime and sweat.*
> (Ibid: 219)

## The Flourishing of Workers' Education

There had to be more to life than this and Read, for one, decided that education was to be his salvation. He began taking adult education courses, especially a course in political economy by Professor David Macgregor and Henry Clay, almost certainly at Swarthmore. Then he managed to borrow some money and enrolled as an undergraduate at Leeds University in 1912. In finding a wealthy sponsor, he was one of the lucky ones but his story shows how important adult education had become for young working people who wanted to transform their lives. In 1870 the Bradford MP and former Quaker, WE Forster, introduced his Education Act, which did a great deal to improve the lot of working class children who, despite the payment by results method and vast classrooms, at least had the beginnings of learning. The Leeds Board of Education was one of the better authorities and fine new schools were built around town. Back in the mid-nineteenth century the Mechanics Institutes had been encouraged by the Leeds manufacturing élite to create a pool of skilled artisans. Despite the efforts of Liberals like Edward Baines who owned the *Leeds Mercury*, this had been strictly business though and only science and technology were taught. Arts and culture had to wait, while any discussion of religion or tuition in politics was firmly excluded. Despite this narrowing of horizons to (the very modern) theme of skills production, the artisan class in Leeds did well and fine careers were made, on occasion the artisans themselves becoming successful business men. But what about those who had missed out?

Many of the more thoughtful turned to militant politics and by the 1880s there was a grass-roots revival of the ethical socialism and trade unionism that had been driven underground by the defeat of Chartism in the 1830s. Industrial trade unions began to organise workers to take action on a mass scale, leading to the great Gas Workers' strike of 1888. Women workers in the tailoring trade also struck in the following year led by the Quaker, Isabella Ford, (who will feature later in this narrative) who became secretary of their newly formed Tailoresses Union (Hannam, 1989: 39). The old Liberal establishment, of which the Fords had been prominent members, began to wonder at the new forces erupting around them. Once content that they had managed to contain a quiescent working class leadership within the fold of Liberalism, they now realised a new militant generation had

sprung from the ground they had unwittingly seeded.
A prominent Liberal J.S. Mathers wrote in 1895:

> *For over five years I have been warning friends that unless the Liberal Party took up and considered these questions [of working class demands] and dealt with them, a great Labour Party would spring up and sweep aside both Tories and Liberals as such and govern for themselves.*
> *(quoted in Woodhouse, 1996: 26)*

As Woodhouse vividly shows, the emergent forces of the new socialism led by Tom Maguire from the slums of the Bank and another Irishman, John Lincoln Mahon, were a small but vital spark leading to the formation of the Independent Labour Party in 1893 and a decade later, as Mathers feared, the Labour Party itself. One of the University extension lecturers sent to Leeds by Cambridge in the 1870s, the Socialist mystic and homosexual rights campaigner, Edward Carpenter, wrote later that it was curious indeed, how influential were the small but innumerable socialist groups around the West Riding in the late nineteenth century: 'the general teaching and ideals of the movement have permeated society in the most remarkable way, and have deeply infected the views of all classes, as well as general literature and even municipal and imperial politics' (quoted in Harrison, 1961: 257). The workers were beginning to educate themselves through their own working class organisations. Often based in the dissenting chapels which were ministered in a very democratic way, in the co-operative movement which by the end of the century was offering 'cradle to grave' services in Leeds, in the newly formed general unions and the Labour Sunday Schools, a new view of how the world wagged was being taught and enthusiastically devoured.

It was abundantly clear that the University extension courses offered by Cambridge and Oxford from the 1870s were not reaching this new class formation and, for the educationally famished, that they offered cake rather than bread. So, under the influence of Benjamin Jowett and the Balliol tradition, university 'settlements' were set up in a number of towns. The most well known of these was Toynbee Hall in the East End of London to which many idealistic young Oxford graduates went to live, encouraged by their tutors like Edward Caird to discover why there was 'so much poverty in the midst of plenty'. These included R. H. Tawney, the social historian who, with others, developed a new intensive form of workers' education called the Tutorial Class which was to become the corner stone of Mansbridge's Workers' Educational Association (WEA), founded as the Association for the Promotion of Higher Education for Working Men in 1903. Many of the tutors came from high Liberal families but were convinced by their experience in adult education classes that working people were no longer represented by the old polity. Many transformed their allegiance, contributing to the first generation of Labour intellectuals. While Quakers were in the vanguard of this movement, it was abundantly clear that women were not going to allow themselves to be excluded from this Brave New World and once again Isabella Ford was at the forefront in Yorkshire and nationally of the National Union of Women's Suffrage Societies. A little later, Mary Gawthorpe, a young Leeds teacher, was to become the national secretary of suffragism's more militant wing, the Women's Social and Political Union (Liddington, 2006).

## The Renaissance of Quakerism and the Origins of Swarthmore

The Religious Society of Friends, or Quakers as they were more commonly known, who had now mostly become a wealthy section of the population, through their devotion to business and frugality, were from the early nineteenth century closely attuned to the deprivation of working people – cocoa manufacture, for example, was associated with the Temperance movement to turn workers away from alcoholic drink. There were many instances of classes run by Quakers, especially for working women in the factories, and the Ford family in Leeds were prime examples of this middle-class philanthropy. Yorkshire Quakers were distinctive in their dedication to social issues and what they called 'the ethic of personal service'. Although now well-integrated into middle-class society they radically disputed its laissez-faire values and became the radical spearhead of what was called the Quaker Renaissance and the 'new Quakerism' of late nineteenth century which the historian of the Rowntree Trust, Mark Freeman, calls a 'triumph of liberal Quakerism' (Freeman, 2004:13). Possibly the most well-known was the Rowntree chocolate-making family, whose 'First Day Schools' for 8–15 year olds were established in York in 1848. Joseph Rowntree, himself, taught in them for 40 years followed by Arnold Rowntree, his nephew, and sons. But for Joseph Rowntree, the establishment of the Adult School Movement was his most valued achievement. It led to a recruitment boost for Quakers of 25-33% and enhanced its social concern. However, as Freeman notes, 'But if these schools gave socially concerned Quakers the opportunity to educate the masses, it also taught them a lot about the way the poor lived, and gave them the sort of contact with the urban working classes that was only rarely, if ever, obtained in other ways' (Freeman, 2004: 16). By 1905 there were 13 Adult Schools in York and 288 in the UK as a whole, whose function was not just to prepare young people for the labour market but to develop the human faculties necessary to a 'progressive civilised community'.

Rather than withdrawing from contemporary society as previous generations had done, the new Quakers engaged with it, inspired by what they called the doctrine of 'inner light'. They took an intense interest in world affairs and York Quakers campaigned against the concentration camps of the Boer War and British naval expansion. Increasingly radicalised, a Socialist Quaker Society was established in 1898, though a less radical group called the Friends' Social Union was established in 1902 under Seebohm Rowntree. All were influenced by the vision of a new practical faith propounded by Joseph Rowntree's eldest son, John Wilhelm Rowntree (1868-1905).

John Wilhelm did much to change the outlook of the Society of Friends in the 1890s and played a leading role in founding its first 'settlement', a hybrid of the Toynbee Hall model and Nicolae Grundtvig's Danish folk high schools, at Woodbrooke near Birmingham. This was envisaged as the hub of the Quaker educational settlements network and initially served as a training ground for settlement wardens. Later it became a more general adult education college for those who wished to play a greater role in their communities. It became very influential for those in Europe who wanted a more secular form of folk high school and, significantly, by 1922 over 33% of its students were foreign (Freeman, 2004; Steele, 2007). Crucial to its success was the income provided by the newly formed Joseph Rowntree Charitable Trust (JRCT) which widely funded ventures with adult school and settlement aims. Joshua Rowntree was Woodbrooke's first Warden and Arnold Rowntree was on the governing body.

The success of Woodbrooke led Friends to ask for a settlement on home soil in Yorkshire, although not necessarily residential. Following John Wilhelm's death in 1905 and in his memory, the important '1905 Committee' was established (Freeman, 2008). In 1909 its chairman, Arnold Rowntree, reported to the JRCT that a joint committee of the Leeds Monthly Meeting and the Yorkshire 1905 Committee had been formed to oversee the establishment of a Friends settlement in Leeds with Gerald K. Hibbert as the Warden and Maurice Rowntree as sub-Warden. Arnold paid the rent while the Trust paid the salaries of Hibbert and Rowntree. The settlement became known as the 'Swarthmore Educational Settlement', and 'was perhaps the logical extension of a tradition of adult education in the city among Quakers and non-Quakers alike' (Ibid).

This was a central commitment for socially aware Quakers and engaged many of the local leading families such as the Fords, Whitings and Harveys as well as the Rowntrees who provided both funding and personnel. The social campaigner Edmund Harvey, later to become a Liberal MP after a brief spell as Warden at Swarthmore, maintained a near life-long interest as Swarthmore's President. He reflected in 1949 that: 'Leeds and York were the first places in England in which this new experiment was begun' by members of the Society of Friends closely associated with Adult School work to carry out the ideal of 'wide Christian citizenship'. Although 12 Clarendon Rd, which housed the new Settlement, was handicapped by the inadequate size of its rooms in a once private residence, Harvey concluded that Swarthmore was a 'not an institution, but a home'. Thousands of students would share in this wide fellowship because it was founded by men and women with 'faith in the Divine possibilities in every human life, without distinction of race or class' (Harvey, 1949).

As Harvey claimed, the creation of the WEA was an important moment for progressive Quakers and Swarthmore quickly affiliated to the Leeds WEA branch formed in 1907. The partnership (with some notable lapses) has lasted the century, the WEA initially contributing to Swarthmore its Oxford University Tutorial Classes in the Social Sciences. The WEA shared the Quaker ethos of personal direction of teachers and the friendly, co-operative atmosphere.

The Settlement at St Mary's, York was also established in the same year as a result of more general social movements rather than as a directly Quaker initiative but was always seen as a kind of sister institution to Swarthmore. Five years later the Beechcroft Settlement in Birkenhead was established in 1914. This had a broader curriculum and was perhaps a more genuine 'community' centre of adult education than Swarthmore or York, which were more specifically aimed at nurturing Adult School leaders. The JRCT continued to fund these and other educational settlements but for many Swarthmore was the jewel in the crown.

### How this history is organised

This Centenary history has been written in a conventional chronological way beginning with the Settlement's origins in 1909 and ending on the edge of 2009, with some thoughts on the future. It has tended to make chapters correspond to the period of tenure of its wardens, who rightly or wrongly have greatly influenced its direction over the century. There is also an appendix listing the wardens and a bibliography of references for those interested in following up the social history of Swarthmore in Leeds and the role of the Friends who created it.

Chapter Two tracks Swarthmore's foundation and early years under its first Warden Gerald K. Hibbert, 1909–1920, detailing its organisation and funding. Initially for the wider education of Adult School (AS) leaders and the spiritual health of the Friends themselves, Swarthmore encouraged non-believers to share in the atmosphere of fellowship. The settlement became a magnet for thoughtful working people determined to understand 'the social problem' and their relationship to it. The First World War had a terrible impact and the infant nearly died. Quakers campaigned actively against the war, Arnold Rowntree as an MP in parliament receiving threats and abuse while the sub-Warden, Maurice Rowntree, was imprisoned for conscientious objection in 1917. Moreover it promoted radically challenging views about the evils of capitalism, which tutors showed did not correspond with the teachings of Jesus. Swarthmore did not get a good press or expect it. It nevertheless became a hub for the Adult School movements in the West Riding, both in hosting visiting Friends and in giving extension lectures and 'Swarthmore Sundays' away from home.

In Chapter Three we cover the turbulent decades from 1919–1939 which were largely tended by Charles Hodgson and Wilfred Allott as Wardens. The Hibberts moved to Ackworth School in 1919 and took a more prominent role in Quakerism nationally. For a short period Edmund Harvey was Warden, prior to seeking election as Liberal MP for Dewsbury. Post-war social and economic conflict escalated into a crisis in belief and many now drawn to Swarthmore were not from the ranks of the faithful. The scholarly and mild mannered Hodgson welcomed them all and with the creation of the Student Guild (later Student Committee), Swarthmore started to become a student democracy. Its reach also now extended via Harvey and Maurice Arnold (briefly an inmate) to classes in Armley Gaol. In 1927 Wilfred Allott returned some of the original dynamism and made Swarthmore a centre of 'internationalism' by boosting the languages programme and welcoming European refugees from persecution. Central to this effort was the redoubtable Martha Steinitz who taught German courses for over three decades. Classes in the arts and crafts also expanded while those in bible study declined. After three decades Swarthmore had changed radically with a broader largely non-religious programme, increased funding from Leeds City Council, and a wide intake of students. Its founding links to Quakerism weakened and although were never lost, a more secular atmosphere prevailed.Collapsed in exhaustion, Allott ended his long stint as Warden early in World War Two and he was succeeded for three years by the sociologist, Desmond Neill, as we see in Chapter Four. Initially the war dampened the Settlement's fire and it might once more have been extinguished were it not, ironically, for the army itself. Swarthmore turned khaki, offering mostly language education for the Army Pay Corps based in Leeds. It heralded a remarkable recovery in fortune and after the war its positive response to reconstruction provided a focal point. Neill was replaced by a former WEA Tutor Organiser, Maurice Hughes, who continued to develop a social purpose agenda and then in 1949 by the more aesthetic Geoffrey Hines. While Hines was rather circumspect about the politics of his predecessors, he established a firm financial base. He also returned a more 'spiritual' dimension to the curriculum while expanding the range of arts subjects particularly literature. Hines was passionate about T.S. Eliot (then courting his wife-to-be Valerie who lived in Weetwood Lane) with whom he corresponded. He also promoted the language programme to become the largest single sector. However, he fell out with the more 'political' WEA and for almost a decade there was no WEA or Leeds University involvement in Swarthmore's programme. Post-war modernity intervened in other ways and Swarthmore was no longer styled a 'Settlement' but a 'Centre'.

In Chapter Five we see the rise of Swarthmore as an Arts Centre under two Wardens, Brian Stapleton and Brian Thompson. This was the cultural revolution of the 1960s when everything changed and the Centre became a haven for creative writers and artists, hosting provocative exhibitions and dramatic scenes (not all on the newly built stage). A succession of Gregory Fellows in Poetry and the Arts were encouraged to teach students. More of Woodhouse Terrace was bought to expand classes and much refurbishment took place. Swarthmore became a substantial property owner receiving help from benefactors like the clothing manufacturer Bernard Lyons (of the Alexandre chain) and the City Council. But in a sense a climacteric had been reached where, financially at least, it would become difficult to call Swarthmore simply an *independent* centre since it now received most of its funding from Leeds – and the piper would ultimately call the tune. It was now more closely integrated into the City's adult education provision and took in overflows from the colleges during the day. Nevertheless the voluntary movement in the shape of the Swarthmore Council and the various committees that ran its affairs, flourished. Money was raised for the refurbishment of its first hall while it maintained its reputation as a friendly place for learning and pushing back boundaries in the Arts.

The radical cultural shifts begun in the 1960s when Britain changed from black and white to colour continued into the 1970s, as we see in Chapter Six. In the 1973 the new Warden (and then Director after 1990) was Martin Russell who served the longest time and presided over some the most critical changes faced by Swarthmore. The open-door policy which had always been the Centre's policy was generously extended and all manner of campaigning groups now found shelter in it. Many hoped that the Russell Report (no relation) of 1973 would initiate a new age for adult education and, although largely ignored by government, it did act as a vital stimulus for those engaged in provision, returning it to what many saw as a long neglected concern for 'the deprived'. The great scourge of the age, however, was mass unemployment, induced by successive governments' monetarist economic policies in the late 1970s and 1980s. Swarthmore both housed and provided educational programmes for unemployment groups and established its own welfare counselling service. While continuing to expand its liberal and practical arts programmes in cooperation with the WEA and the University, Swarthmore intensified its own social concern. Perhaps the most interesting new programme was Fresh Starts which was one of the first new style 'Access' to Further and Higher Education courses complete with crèche and counselling. Another achievement was the succession of creative Arts Fellowships funded by Yorkshire Arts which brought members into active relationship with practising artists. Spurred on by the success of its applications to the new sources of funding opening up, Swarthmore also secured funds to build a brand new hall to replace the one built in the 1950s. By the turn of the 1990s however a serious financial crisis meant new mainstream funding had to be found. The Further and Higher Education Act (1992) ironically threw a lifeline and Swarthmore successfully applied for majority funding to be transferred to the newly created Further Education Funding Council (FEFC). However, it came at a cost: the large scale accreditation of the programme – a policy Swarthmore Council had long resisted – and Business Plans.

Chapter Seven surveys the last act of Swarthmore's century. Driven by funding changes it has been obliged to become a limited company and an entrepreneurial venture (but of a distinctly social kind). It has acquired a substantial administrative staff to deal with the various sources of income, the paraphernalia of accreditation and the priority groups at which it is targeted. Annual reports began to look more like company statements. Its annual income soared at one point, in 2005, to nearly one million pounds (compared with the £900 of its first year) with a comparable wage bill. It has since had to cut back, and lose staff, but the programme has remained remarkably buoyant. Day-time provision is dominated by provision for priority deprived and disabled groups, while there is still a lively 'self-funding' arts and crafts evening programme. Sadly, both languages and the close partnership with the WEA have all but disappeared from the programme and the voluntarist engagement lessened. Links with the Society of Friends, at one time almost vestigial, have however been renewed in the use of the Airton Meeting House and the homeless memorial services.

We conclude this history with some thoughts about the future. It is a testament to its redoubtable spirit that Swarthmore has survived, almost uniquely, its first hundred years and even flourished as a centre for education and fellowship in the face of adversity. It never ceases to plan for the future and is already shaping its next century. We hope that this history will reveal how it continues to provide an inspiring model for the very best kind adult education in the challenging years ahead.

Gerald Kenway Hibbert, The first Swarthmore Warden, 1909–1919

## CHAPTER 2

# 'A Place for Friends', 1909-1920

### Foundations

The great crowd forming at Woodhouse Square, on the evening of 25 September 1909 had arrived in the expectation of something vitally new to the life of Leeds. It was 'a huge crush' according to Hewitson (1959) and people were not disappointed to hear a rousing speech from one of the main authors of the project, Arnold Rowntree, Joseph Rowntree's nephew, on the need for loving fellowship in life and the right of all working men and women to a decent education in order to understand the world in all its grim beauty. The building outside which the crowd gathered was not, however, the Georgian Terrace at the lower end of Woodhouse Square that was to become so familiar to thousands over the century but higher up the hill at number 12 Clarendon Rd. Though an impressive building (designed by George Corson for Herbert Rayner in 1868) it still looked more like the home of a prosperous Leeds burgher than an educational institution. But it was precisely this *homeliness* that the founders attempted to instil into the educational life of the 'Settlement'.

Swarthmore was to be the first non-residential educational Settlement founded by the Yorkshire Quakers and funded by them. Arnold Rowntree himself paid the rent on 12 Clarendon Rd and the JRCT paid the wages of the Warden, Gerald Hibbert, and his Assistant Lecturer, Maurice Rowntree. Hibbert's wife Wilhelmina, although unpaid, took a great responsibility in running the settlement and played an active role in teaching women, as she had done previously at Woodbrooke College (see previous chapter). The project owed a great deal to the energies of three Yorkshire Quaker families, the Whitings, Fords and Harveys. William Harvey and William Whiting had set up a committee to raise money from subscriptions from wealthy Friends for what they thought of as a more advanced form of adult education than the worthy but limited literacy work of the Adult Schools. In particular they wanted a place to train leaders for Adult School (AS) work, both in bible studies and in social issues about which Friends were becoming radically concerned. Gervase Ford became the Settlement's treasurer for many years while his sister Isabella was a very active Council member.

Wardens frequently create a distinctive identity at the settlements and centres they run and Hibbert demonstrably set the tone for his successors. As the first Warden he tried to create not only a home to cultivate AS leaders but a place where all those committed to social reform through educational and 'Christian' ideals might be welcome. Recalling the period in 1949 Hibbert noted that Swarthmore was 'definitely (though not narrowly) a Quaker organisation' and owed a great deal to its partnerships with the WEA and the University. He tried to marry the twin concerns of biblical understanding and the study of social problems in order to illuminate how the teachings of the bible might be applied to the grievous state of contemporary society. Swarthmore, he said, set out with high aims:

**Gerald Kenway Hibbert**

Warden 1909-1919 with his wife Wilhelmina. Formerly a Baptist minister. Having established the tone of social concern at Swarthmore, left in 1919 to become Head of Ackworth School and becomes a very influential figure in 20th century Quakerism. From 1930 Reader in Quakerism at Woodbrooke - influenced the revival of religious education under Henry and Lucy Cadbury at Woodbrooke.

Clarendon Road, Leeds, site of the original Swarthmore Settlement

> *to assist in self education; to provide an evening college for the otherwise college-less; to be a home centre for men and women who wish to be serviceable; to create and cement friendships; to guide active workers; to inspire lives; to welcome visitors with open doors; to reach out helpfully to other Yorkshire centres.* (Hibbert, 1911: 2-3)

Hibbert was a deeply religious man, although his form of religion, a very political Quakerism, might puzzle religious fundamentalists today. For him religion was inseparable from the needs of humanity and had nothing to do with religious dogmatism:

> *Quakerism looks on life as a whole: it cannot see religion as belonging to one department and reform to another. It sees that a religion which does not issue in social reform is a bastard religion, and not the religion of Christ; while social service divorced from religion loses it vitality and soon withers as a branch when severed from the trunk'.* (Hibbert, 1911: 12)

So no religion without social reform and no reform without religion, but the key was love: 'if Christ be rightly interpreted, the worst sins against God are those most injurious to man. Love is the supreme orthodoxy; indifference to the needs of humanity the only heterodoxy' (Hibbert, 1911:14). But other lesser things must not be mistaken for religion itself:

> *The glory of the Settlement Movement is that it emphasizes religion as fundamental. It uses the word "religion" in a broad and comprehensive sense. It sees the danger of putting second things first, so it cannot exalt literature or social service at the expense of religion. Rather does it see in all true literature and in all social service worthy of the name, simply an expression of that religious spirit which had been man's constant guide and companion in his upward climb.* (Hibbert, 1911:15)

Committed to extending the mission of Swarthmore beyond Leeds, Hibbert spent much time recruiting outside the settlement throughout Yorkshire, attracting people who were, according to a later Annual Report (AR), 'readjusting their views on religious matters in the light of new Biblical and historical knowledge' (21st Annual Report, p2). Increasingly urgent attention to war and peace was drawn in Hibbert's lectures between 1913 and 1914, as the clouds gathered.

The Assistant Warden and Lecturer was Maurice Rowntree, described as an 'adventurous spirit' from his frequent travels in foreign countries to observe and draw lessons their social conditions. Later he would give a course at Swarthmore on what he had seen in his travels in the USA, drawing attention to the truly appalling conditions he had found in the stockyards. The Hibberts and Rowntree were aided by up to five resident Leeds University students, on the Toynbee Hall model. They were funded by another Quaker foundation, the Flounders Institute, who also donated the nucleus of a library to Swarthmore. One of the students was Wilfrid Allott, who had an Exhibition to the University in 1911 and succeeded as warden in 1922. Voluntary support was encouraged, beginning with a gardening committee in 1910 and the gloomy patch of sooty dirt to the side of the house soon blossomed into a garden of tranquillity and beauty in which classes were frequently held.

## Educational Provision

So what kind of educational provision was on offer in these heady days for the 213 or so eager learners who devoted their evenings to study? The bias of the classes was religious (four out of the original seven classes) while the other classes were on social affairs. These included Economics and a course especially for women on Women Work and Wages. There was also a course on Life and Thought in the East. A key element of educational provision, however, was Swarthmore's cooperation with the Leeds WEA branch which had been formed two years earlier in 1907. Still very much in its pioneering days, the WEA branch had been formed by trade unionists, co-operators (members of the Leeds Industrial Co-operative Society) and Leeds University academics, many of whom had long experience in the University Extension movement in either Oxford or Cambridge. 'Mansbridge came to bless us' said Hibbert later, meaning Albert Mansbridge, the founder of the WEA, who had done so much to secure the support of the universities in its work and reassure the trade unions that this was not just middle-class ideology (Hibbert, 1949).

### Maurice Rowntree

Sub Warden 1909–1917. Appointed lecturer and assistant in 1909 but, militantly 'socialistic' and pacifist, imprisoned for conscientious objection 1917. Son of Joseph Rowntree's cousin Joshua, a prominent Quaker educational reformer, who had been the first Warden of the pioneering Woodbrooke residential settlement. As Joshua's son 'the trust (JRCT) took a great interest in his welfare and future prospects' (Freeman, 2004: 33). Always itching to move on, however, he left Leeds for a while to found a Settlement in Scarborough in 1913 but returned to teach at Swarthmore. In 1917 he was imprisoned for conscientious objection and subsequently became involved with Dick Sheppard's Peace Pledge Union to 'renounce war and never again to support another' in 1934.

It was with this university connection, which would guarantee quality and seriousness allied with the working-class democratic spirit of the WEA, that the founders of Swarthmore hoped its education provision would be grounded. From the beginning it was the WEA's very popular Oxford University Tutorial class of three years in Economic History taught by Henry Clay, which was regarded as exemplary. When retiring from the presidency of the WEA in 1958, Clay who later became a leading economist and was knighted for his contribution to public service, claimed it was among the happiest of his experiences. The Oxford Committee that oversaw adult Tutorial Classes agreed that a very high level of work had been done, *easily equivalent to undergraduate standard*. A key element of the class's success was the 'Book Box', jealously guarded by a member of the class who became the class librarian, issuing books and making sure they were returned. Oxford loaned 42 books for the 29 members of the class, who wrote a very impressive total of 212 essays between them in one year (an average of seven per student). The WEA may in addition have contributed to the first tutorial class on Theology run by Hibbert himself. The defining aspect of the 'Tutorial' class was that it should run over three years, gradually deepening into the nature of the subjects studied and responding to the particular interests of the students themselves, who would suggest topics and ways of approaching their study. The classes were usually two hours long, the first hour being devoted to the tutor's presentation, hardly a lecture, on the theme or problem for the night, while the second hour was given over to class discussion. Class members would talk about their own experiences of working life and political activity, offering them up for debate by the rest of the class and the tutor's specialist scrutiny. This form of education was not so much unknown inside universities as simply neglected and bore some influence from Quaker meetings. Its importance was such that many of the pioneer tutors from Oxford like Clay (and R.H. Tawney, though not in Swarthmore) felt that they learned more from the students than they taught them. For those who did not want to commit themselves to three years study of this kind, Swarthmore offered one-year classes along similar themes but of a less demanding nature. Tutors were paid £80 per course, half of which was paid by Swarthmore, the rest by Oxford.

The infant University of Leeds had received it charter only five years previously in 1904 and was not yet in a position to offer

Maurice Rowntree, Swarthmore Sub Warden, 1909–1917

Tutorial courses on the Oxford or Cambridge models. It was still finding its feet as a university catering for the utilitarian needs of local manufacturers but trying to integrate an Arts and Humanities curriculum. As a general condition of moving to full university status it was required to establish Arts faculties, which it did as often as not by appointing as Professors many who had been active the university extension movement. Early luminaries included Professors David Macgregor, A.J. Grant, and Frederic W. Moorman, who immediately took active roles in both the WEA and Swarthmore.

Classes were held in the evenings from Monday to Friday with the exception of Thursday which was a 'free night', although in fact it was used to train prospective Adult School leaders about 'Vital Points in the Adult School Lesson'. In the first year 1909–1910 Swarthmore offered a modest range of classes expressing its ideal of marrying bible study to a concern for understanding social conditions. In the spirit of Quaker scepticism and undogmatic search for truth, Hibbert offered a course on Is Christianity True? as well as others on the Old Testament, New Testament, Quakerism, and Modern Prophets and their message. From Leeds University, Prof. David Macgregor combined with Maurice Rowntree to teach a course on Economics and the Poor Law, which led to an indictment on the factory system. There was a practical Junior and Primary teachers' class and, for women, a class on Child life and Labour. The beginning of another important line of tuition was the first language class in German which was held in 1914 on the eve of the Great War. This stemmed from a previous class on Germany and her People in 1910 given by the Warden in which he established that the key principle of language teaching should be its grounding in the context of the culture and spirit of the language speakers, that so impressed the HMI, who was at the time John Dover Wilson, the Shakespearian scholar (Wilson, 1928). In the same year a French class was started.

On Saturdays Swarthmore hosted visits from neighbouring Adult Schools in the West Riding, which were in turn complemented by 'extra-mural' visits to them by Maurice Rowntree and Geoffrey Hibbert. Although evening classes were conventionally seen as autumn and winter activities, the Warden was keen to continue the educational year through the spring and summer. In April 1910, Swarthmore offered the first of its summer classes of Nature Studies led by Richard Swain, who was a science teacher at the Friends' Rawdon School and who was widely held to be one of the Centre's most gifted tutors. It was symptomatic of its approach that education should not begin and end with the formal class but should continue within a new kind of sociability. So Swain started a Natural History Society where members met for informal discussion, observation, rambles and guest lectures, beginning a tradition of clubs generated by Swarthmore activities.

**Richard Swain**

Assistant Warden 1917–1921. Science Teacher at Friends' Rawdon School. Introduces a new syllabus including 'Human Geography' and the 'Science of Common Life' and English Poetry 1918. His 'breezy personality and youthful enthusiasm' inspire all. Death in the summer 1921 but 'leaves many a life brighter and better'.

Swarthmore Specimen Syllabus from 1910

A SPECIMEN SYLLABUS:—

MONDAY—
 7-30.—Women's Class: "Child Life and Labour," Miss S. K. Findlay, M.A.
 7-45.—" Is Christianity True ? " G. K. Hibbert, M.A.
TUESDAY—Coaching as desired.
 7-45.—" The Old Testament : Its Living Value for To-Day,"
       A. Neave Brayshaw, B.A.
 7-45.—" Economics and Poor Law," Professor D. H. MacGregor, M.A., and
       Maurice L. Rowntree, B.A.
WEDNESDAY—
 4-0.—New Testament Class, G. K. Hibbert, M.A.
 8-0.—Primary Teachers' Class, Maurice L. Rowntree, B.A.
THURSDAY—
 2-30.—New Testament Class, Maurice L. Rowntree, B.A.
 7-30.—The Wardens At Home to all Students.
 8-0.—Next Sunday's Adult School Lesson ; "Ways of Teaching ;" Question
       and Answer.
 8-0.—Junior Teachers' Class.
FRIDAY—Coaching as desired.
 7-45.—"Quakerism: Its Story and Inner Meaning," G. K. Hibbert, M.A.
SATURDAY—
 †4-15.—" Modern Prophets and their Message " (2nd Saturday in each month).
 ‡5-15.—Tea.
 6-15.—The Event of the Week.
 7-30.—" Germany and its People," Maurice L. Rowntree, B.A. (every other week).
       On the alternate Saturday nights, Book Talks, Lantern Lectures,
       Music, etc.

 † The following are the subjects for this term :—" John Ruskin," by James H. Heighton, Bradford. " Richard Jefferies," by Percy Fletcher, York. " Charles Kingsley," by Maurice L. Rowntree.
 ‡ Tea (price 6d.) will be provided every Saturday, for all who give notice the preceding day. Coffee (or cocoa) and biscuits are provided every week-night, about 9 o'clock, price 1d.
 BOOKS.—A list of inexpensive text-books will be supplied to every student. Copies of these books may be seen (and purchased) at Swarthmore.
 FEES.—1/6 per subject per person for the term of three months ; 2/6 for two subjects per person for the term of three months ; 3/6 for composition fee for all except specially advertised lectures. These fees include use of library.

The ideal of fellowship was central to the founders' ambitions, which drew on Mazzini's often cited insistence that 'the group method of study and the social amenities of the Common Room help to fulfil [the] idea of education through fellowship' (Gillman, 1916: 14) and intellectual life was nothing without co-operative learning. Mazzini's educational philosophy was best expressed by his a pre-eminent follower, Jane Addams (1860-1935) the founder of the American Settlement movement and first American woman to win the Nobel Prize:

> *Intellectual life requires for its expansion and manifestation the influences and assimilation of the interests and affections of others. Mazzini, that greatest of all democrats, who broke his heart over the condition of the South European peasantry, said: "Education is not merely a necessity of true life by which the individual renews his vital force in the vital force of humanity; it is a Holy Communion with generations dead and living, by which he fecundates all his faculties. When he is withheld from this Communion for generations, as the Italian peasant has [...] been, we say, 'He is like a beast of the field; he must be controlled by force.'" Even to this it is sometimes added that it is absurd to educate him, immoral to disturb his content. We stupidly use the effect as an argument for a continuance of the cause. It is needless to say that a Settlement is a protest against a restricted view of education.* (Addams, 1910: 428)

By the end of its third year it was clear Swarthmore was becoming confident of its role and abilities, such that Hibbert later claimed: 'Working men acquired rich personalities as they added culture to a harder experience of life than that of the average graduate' many taking up public positions of service. It announced itself as a non-residential college conducted as a 'home' for all men and women who 'wish to be of use to their fellows' and opened its annual report with statements from students on the value of Swarthmore to them personally, such as: 'the happiest stroke in theological studies that I have made', 'more of a home than an institution', an 'indefinable uplift' and for another a place where she could develop a 'sense of beauty and uplift'. There is already a feeling from students that it offered an answer to a long cherished ideal and the entrance into a larger life but one that would require 'mental effort' and 'eager questing and analysis' – sentiments many times re-echoed over the next century. The third year had been the most fruitful so far. Following the success of the History of Religion course the previous year, Oxford University agreed to provide a Tutorial class in History and Economics by one of its most committed tutors, Henry Clay (who later became a leading economist and major figure in the adult education movement). Such Oxford Tutorial classes were to be seen as the serious core to Swarthmore's provision and carried on for many years, eventually being superseded by those from Leeds.

The following year, 1912–13, Swarthmore announced its object as to equip all those engaged in religious and social work with an education. Enrolment had slipped slightly to 164 but attendance at classes had risen to 180 (due to individuals taking more than one class). These in turn became 'missionaries to other parts of the West Riding', where 'Swarthmore Sundays' were held. Swarthmore was already broadening out and extending its reach and reading circles centred mostly on bible subjects were established. Rumours of war, however, raised the temperature and special attention was paid to counteracting militarism and the 'education of the democracy'. Hibbert's Tutorial class on Religious Philosophy 'deepened' the understanding of Adult School tutors who were Swarthmore's core constituency on the early days. This was complemented by the continuation of a second tutorial under Henry Clay on Industry, History and Economics which confirmed the commitment to understanding social problems. Maurice Rowntree gave a class on Social Problems and a new strand was opened with classes on Nature Study given by Nora Dudley and Richard Swain. The tireless Hibbert offered further classes on religious themes including Revelations of the Great Souls: Augustine, Bunyan, Fox and Wesley, the Teachings of Jesus, and the Early Church. Hibbert even managed to squeeze in a class on British Novelists, marking the opening of another thematic study for Swarthmore, that of English literature (itself related to bible study). Alongside this opening to the humanities more generally, were classes in the Beginnings of Modern England, Civics, and Religion and Science given by Prof. W. H. Bragg, and one on International Policy. A course on Hygiene in the Modern Home seemed, conventionally, to be aimed at women.

As an introduction to Swarthmore for new members, special lectures were offered at the beginning of term and on Saturday afternoons. These included two on Karl Marx in April and September given by Herbert Wood of the Woodbrooke Settlement, no doubt further convincing a sceptical local press (Yorkshire Conservative Newspapers) that it was up to no good. Other special lectures included one on the Rights of Man in Nineteenth Century Thought and the radical Quaker poet John Greenleaf Whittier. Prof. Charles Vaughan of Leeds University gave a provocative lecture on Thomas Carlyle as a political and social thinker, praising his early career as democratic thinker but utterly condemning his later Hero Worship ideology. The current form of this odious philosophy, claimed Vaughan, was Nietzsche's 'utterly disgusting' doctrine of the 'Over-man' (*Yorkshire Weekly Post*, 21.1.1911). This was probably a swipe at the fashionable Nietzscheanism formerly popularised by Alfred Orage at the Leeds Arts Club in Woodhouse Lane and then in his journal the *New Age* in London. (Steele, 1990)

A visiting Frenchwoman, entranced by what she found at Swarthmore, reported that she attended a course in English novelists to improve her English and understanding of the English and discovered the 'wit, humour and kindly optimism' of the Quakers who were 'intelligent folk with whom one can converse freely and without restraint'. Other prestigious visitors came to give their blessing including the newly established Vice Chancellor of Leeds University, Michael Sadler. Later knighted for his services to education, he was one of the leading figures in British education and great patron of the arts. A Yorkshireman, Sadler was married to the eldest daughter of another Quaker, Charles Harvey, who was a wealthy Barnsley linen manufacturer. At school in Rugby he was a contemporary of R.H. Tawney and William Temple and like them was deeply influenced by John Ruskin and Arnold Toynbee as an undergraduate at Oxford. As chair of the Oxford Extension Committee (responsible for adult education classes) he pushed forward a major expansion of its activities. As an art patron while Vice Chancellor at Leeds, Sadler was responsible for promoting the career of the painter Jacob Kramer and collecting some of Wassily Kandinsky's earliest abstract paintings, some of which he hung publicly in the university. (Access to his huge collection of contemporary art stimulated both Henry Moore to work with abstract form and Herbert Read to find a language for talking about it, see Steele, 1990).

However, despite his general sympathy for the workers' movement and careful cultivation of its leaders in the West Riding, Sadler fell out of favour because of his opposition to the 1913 Municipal Workers Strike in which, with poor judgement, he sent students to strike-break. This brought outraged rebukes from his colleagues such as Arthur Greenwood, David Macgregor and Henry Clay who demanded his resignation from the WEA, claiming it was serious betrayal of working people. Sadler eventually recanted and was accepted back into the fold.

## War or Peace?

The onset of the Great War confronted Swarthmore with its first test of character. As a devoutly pacifist organisation the Quakers argued forcefully about the evils of war in many quarters. How would Swarthmore respond to the patriotic call to arms? Significantly, it was by announcing its own version of 'national service' and its 1914–15 (6th year) Annual Report bore the legend 'Training for national service' for which it wanted to develop not soldiers but an 'enlightened citizenship'. The war robbed Swarthmore of many students but class attendance still held at around 180 and standards kept high. More courses focused on social and political history including the curiously entitled Foundations of National Greatness, based on the book on the same name by Charles Braithwaite but not in the least an inflammatory piece of jingoism. Braithwaite, on the contrary, was an impassioned reformer and in 1916 praised the efforts made by Swarthmore and the other newly created Settlements such as that at St Mary's in York for 'the stress it laid on fellowship and education' (Gilman, 1916: 55). He disagreed entirely with the fashionable mantra that national greatness was the result of the achievements of a small minority of militaristic Great Men. On the contrary, he argued, it was dependent on social harmony and collective effort – but since this was now grievously fractured by the forces of commerce, it had to be healed by education. He believed in a specific version of the class divide:

> *The chasm between the educated and the uneducated is probably the chief line separation in English life today. I think in practice that it is more important than differences in means or position. It is easy to get on with any man of education and outlook similar to your own, because you have numbers of points of contact with his mind'.*
> (Quoted in Gilman, 1916: 55)

Like Addams he valued Mazzini's ideal of 'education by association' but significantly he agreed with the great Indian poet Rabindranath Tagore about the freedom to think without fear and the need for a place where the 'clear stream of reason has not lost its way into the dreary desert of dead habit' (Ibid.). For Braithwaite, 'fellowship' was the goal which would overcome 'differences of class and sect and condition' to create a unity of life 'not of any material uniformity but of a common spirit of life animating all' and by fellowship in the education of mind and soul we can make 'surer steps to the City of God'. Another of Braithwaite's sayings characterised the teaching at Swarthmore and sister institutions not as dogmatic instruction but inspiration and illumination where:

> *The leader tries to stir faculties to action, to wake the mind and soul into vision and discovery, bringing men to those red-letter hours of experience when they become aware of a new truth, in all the freshness and beauty which attends it at its moment of revelation.* (Ibid.)

Such was the Christian social radicalism that energised the Swarthmore pioneers and gave them the strength to resist the clamour of war raging through Leeds (and enriching many of its manufacturers).

By the middle of the war, 1915–16 (7th year), Swarthmore had subtly changed the legend on its annual report to 'Preparing for *international* service' quoting Sadler on the 'readiness to sacrifice selfish interests to the public service'. This again set down a marker for its future orientation which came to fruition between the wars, with a commitment to international service in religious and social work. From the point of view of the Warden, the war seemed to have created a deep earnestness for study and the influx of a wider group of students displayed Swarthmore's increasing influence in Leeds and the West Riding. Swarthmore students were now giving leadership in local Adult Schools, Lecture schools, Sunday schools and study circles, leading to deeper knowledge of what for them was the Holy Trinity of the Bible, economics and (English) literature. What it called 'Extension Work' was now carried out at Brighouse and in the Rowntrees' model village of New Earswick. International and national reconstruction work was now prevalent in discussions and in the essential monthly devotional meetings. These were themselves hailed by Gilman as a significant experiment in adult education that combined distinctive features of a Lecture School with a Quaker meeting in which 'students can freely speak their minds and state difficulties which in other surroundings they dare not express' (Gilman, 1916: 17).

But the war had done even more to sharpen the radical political purpose of the Settlement. An increasing urgency shaped the programme with classes like the Rise and Development of the British People, which traced the 'democratic ideal' in British politics to the rise of the Labour Movement. This was taught by Maurice Rowntree, who seems to have been largely responsible for the more radical tone. He followed on with a course on War and the Social Order in Autumn 1915, for which the syllabus noted, 'A true ideal of peace must embrace the class struggle as well as international war'. In the following year, the class continued with an examination of the ethics of the capitalist system and how best to move towards 'a system which more truly promotes and expresses the ideal of human brotherhood at home and abroad'. Tragically however, Rowntree was refused exemption under the Military Services Act from serving in the forces and arrested in February 1917. He served the rest of the war in Armley Gaol, sewing mailbags and the seeds of education, which were further cultivated after the war by Edmund Harvey.

Tributes from conscientious objectors and serving soldiers and others flowed into Swarthmore for its 'help, strength and joy'. But as far as he was concerned, Rowntree was only trying to place the teachings of Jesus and the New Testament into a contemporary context which, in the midst of such wealth, seemed to condemn so many to a life of poverty. In a less dramatic way Gerald Hibbert appeared to be taking the same approach, teaching courses on such topics as the Foundations of our Faith and Present Day Problems for Quakerism, which addressed such issues as how to resolve the relationship between outward authority and the 'Inward Light'. He inquired into the basis for the Quaker Peace Testimony, the individual and the state, national service and the 'Competitive System'. Hibbert also subtly made connections between the Old Testament and contemporary life with a course on Hebrew Prophets and their message for today.

This broadened into a significant new direction for Swarthmore, with classes and study circles on International Relations in concert with the Council for the Study of International Relations, recently set up by Arthur Greenwood and David Macgregor from Leeds University. From this time on the ideals of 'Europe' and internationalism become recurrent themes in Swarthmore's vocabulary, which, linked with the growth of language classes, especially in French and German, begin to offer another strand to Swarthmore's identity. Greenwood, an economics lecturer and shortly to become a Labour MP, gave one of the special opening lectures on Nationalism and Internationalism. Greenwood was shortly to play an important role in the Ministry of Reconstruction, where he became secretary to the Adult Education Committee, which recommended permanent funding for adult education. Further concern for social problems were shown with an opening lecture by a Factory Inspector, a Miss Sadler, on Women and Children in Factories.

### The New Era

By the final year of the war Swarthmore had orientated itself towards the problem of post-war reconstruction, its annual report for 1917–18 bearing the legend 'The New Era', which would require 'social effort inspired by the light within'. Swarthmore seems to have flourished despite the war or perhaps because of its principled objection to warfare. The report notes it had never had such a splendid spirit and talked about a new social ideal requiring 'reform or revolution'. But, in the year of the 'atheistic' Soviet Revolution, it never failed to emphasise the centrality of deep systematic study of the bible and social history to social reform. Women had finally won the vote and this extension of the franchise to women, equally revolutionary in its way, brought a course on civic responsibilities and Isabella Ford gave the opening lecture in 1918 on Women and the Vote. In addition the Settlement hosted two conferences on Housing led by the social campaigner, Seebohm Rowntree and a course of lectures on Christian Evangelism.

What kind of people came to Swarthmore? Hibbert again gives the answer: there were many shades of thought including, 'Anglicans, Methodists, Unitarians-Theosophists, Faith Healers, Christian Scientists-Conservatives, Liberals, Socialists – we have had them all' (Hibbert 1911: 3). Swarthmore, he

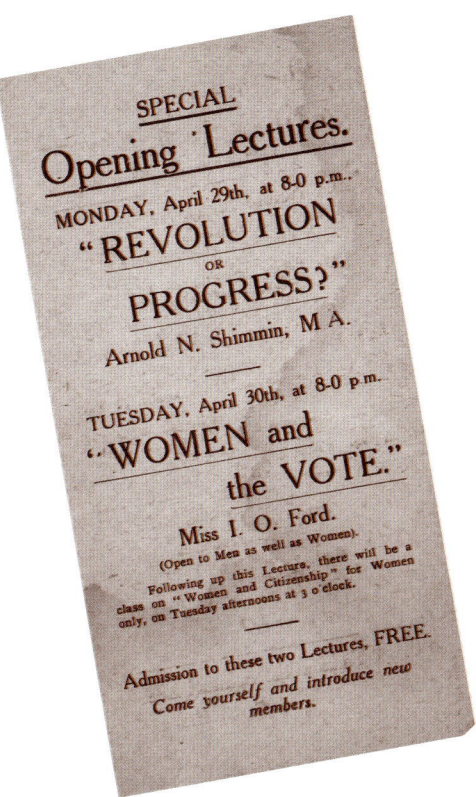

Front cover and inside pages from the 1918 Swarthmore Settlement programme of lectures

claimed, provided a common platform 'where under sympathetic guidance, extremists can define their position without losing their temper' which resulted after a year or so in 'growing toleration and mutual respect' (Ibid.). Central to this ideal of harmony was the understanding that education for fellowship did not begin and end in the classroom but continued after. So, following the classes which usually ran between 7.45 and 9.00pm there was a 'Penny Supper' in the common room, a hymn and short period of devotion.

Social concerns were, of course, not the only diet for Swarthmore's eager learners, for it would have made them very dull. Art began to be noticed more and the radical new Director of Leeds Art Gallery, Frank Rutter, gave a sparkling opening lecture. Rutter had been attracted to Leeds because of Sadler's art patronage and the great success of the Leeds Arts Club. (But he too could not stay out of trouble especially when his feminist wife secured the escape of the suffragette, Lillian Lenton, when she was temporarily released from prison under the 'Cat and Mouse' Acts. See Liddington, 2006). The study of literature and philosophy too was gaining ground, Hibbert giving courses on the Greek tragedians and classical philosophers, while there were special lectures on Dante, Goethe's Faust, Tennyson and Whittier by Frank Moorman. Related classes on public speaking and expression also freely utilised literary texts and Swarthmore members were tutored not only in the deep social issues of the day but how to express themselves eloquently in public. As part of Swarthmore's outreach work, an extension reading circle was proposed for Wakefield colliers who had never read a book before, although it never materialised. Another element that was making itself felt was science. With his appointment to the Assistant Warden's job in Maurice Rowntree's absence, Swain lectured successively on the natural cycle of the year, the Science of Common Life and Our Island Home which he described in the syllabus as 'a simple course on "Human Geography"'. Interestingly, in this Swain was pursuing a relatively new form of study, pioneered by the great French geographer (and prominent anarchist) Elisée Reclus and his friend the eminent Scottish educationist Patrick Geddes which was closer to sociology (Steele, 2007).

An increasingly important element which really knitted the social fabric together were Swarthmore's recreational activities, especially rambles and nature study walks that took place over the weekend, the Washburn Valley becoming a favourite place for excursions. As we shall see, this side of Swarthmore's activities was self-organised by students and shortly crystallised into the Student's Guild which formed the basis of the student democracy that Swarthmore was to become.

## Management and Money

How was this hive of activity managed? Although the Yorkshire Friends oversaw the whole project – still regarded as an 'experiment' – there was an appointed (not yet elected) governing body called the Swarthmore Council. In 1919 this consisted of a rather unwieldy group of 43 people including the Warden, his wife and Assistant. The Harvey, Whiting and Rowntree families were well-represented and for the University of Leeds, Prof. A. J. Grant, one of the leading European historians of the day. Other influential figures included George Thompson, the WEA Yorkshire District Secretary, who oversaw the university Joint Committee programme of Tutorial classes and Albert Tallant, a Labour city councillor. Tallant's son, Alfred, succeeded him on both Leeds City and Swarthmore councils until the 1970s. Although largely drawn from the ranks of Friends, many non-Quakers were invited to take part. Women were surprisingly well in evidence, contributing 15 councillors, including Isabella Ford. Councillors would serve for three years before having to stand down.

Financially, Quaker trusts and families provided most of the income. This was before the days of large-scale grant-aiding by the state or local council – although for the first time during the war there was a small government grant of £8 4/6d for practical subjects. Of the Income of £887 4/6d in 1919–1920 (a figure that remained relatively steady over the founding decade) two thirds came from subscriptions mostly from wealthy Quakers while £112 came from the Woodhead Trust. Student fees from the 200 or so students, again a relatively constant figure over the decade, contributed to less than one twelfth of income at £70, while the only other significant source of income was the fee of £106, paid by Leeds University for its boarders. How was it spent? Naturally the biggest expenditure was on staff who received £382, the other large sums going on rent and rates of £130 and housekeeping of £134, firmly under the control of Wilhelmina Hibbert.

The government grant may well have covered a class of Physical Exercises and Free Movements for women, advertised on a handbill as a 'class for Simple and Systematic Exercises for Women, designed to meet the National need for increased mental and physical vigour' – chaps presumably were getting their exercise elsewhere.

How could this founding period be summed up? Such was Swarthmore's importance as an adult education experiment that it achieved prominence in Frederick Gilman's book on *Workers and Education* (1916) from which we have quoted and Swarthmore also gave evidence to the Ministry of Reconstruction's Committee on Adult education of its 'humanising of education'. In the famous *1919 Report* subsequently published by the Ministry, which laid down the pattern for public funding of adult education, Swarthmore was specifically (though not altogether reliably) discussed (Great Britain, 1980). Under Gerald Hibbert, who was shortly to depart to become the Head of the Quaker Ackworth School near Barnsley, Swarthmore had begun life as an educational centre for leaders of Adult Schools' bible classes. It stressed how bible study should be related to contemporary social concerns and how to interpret Quakerism in a modern context. While Hibbert brought a strong vein of spirituality to the task, Maurice Rowntree expressed it in a lively political radicalism that ultimately forced him to reside at his majesty's pleasure for a period. They were not afraid to discuss the revolutionary theories of Marxism and the significance of 'class struggle'.

However the core educational grounding was in the Tutorial Courses at first provided by Oxford and then Leeds Universities in partnership with the WEA in Social and Economic History. The period saw the rooting of internationalism through discussion of foreign countries and cultures and the teaching of languages that was to become a mainstream feature in the inter-war years. The study of nature and the role of science in human affairs grew as a rebuke to biblical literalism, while art and aesthetic appreciation made a strong appearance. Women were always given special consideration, and although initially this conservatively positioned them as the 'angels of hearth', responsible for home economics and hygiene, a vein of feminist radicalism began to emerge as with Margaret C. Tree's special lecture on Women and Politics in January 1919 and Isabella Ford's influence in the

Council. Sociability played an essential part and the cultivation of a homely atmosphere and 'fellowship', expressed in rambling and informal discussion, marked Swarthmore as something more than just another educational institution, an identity it bore well into its century. Tragically, 'One of Swarthmore's best friends' Prof. Frederick Moorman (the folklorist discoverer of 'Ilkla Moor baht 'at') died while trying to rescue his son from drowning in the River Wharfe. The Hibberts and Maurice Rowntree moved on. Who was to guide Swarthmore into the New Era?

## CHAPTER 3

# Social Justice and International Understanding, 1920–1939

With the ungodly carnage of the war, interest in Bible study was waning and students looked increasingly for more material explanations for their situation. The *1919 Report* on Reconstruction initiated a new age in adult education and Swarthmore was keen to see how it fitted in (Great Britain, 1981). The report's secretary was Arthur Greenwood who, as noted in the last chapter, was formerly a young economics lecturer at Leeds University. Greenwood had lectured frequently at Swarthmore and other settlements including St Mary's at York, before becoming a Labour MP. Against the wishes of the WEA nationally, Greenwood had pushed forward the creation of the Yorkshire District of the WEA in 1914. Swarthmore Council had to decide on whether it should embark on more socially advanced education. Seeing there was a need to create more formal links with the other Settlements – now in Liverpool, in Lemington on Tyne and York, for example, as well as the residential settlements at Woodbrooke and Fircroft – two of its founders went on to establish the Educational Settlements Association (ESA) in 1929. The *1919 Report* had urged universities to establish extra-mural departments for adult education, as part of a national system of adult education, along with the WEA and the Adult Schools, aimed at the serious education of the citizen. But, as Fieldhouse notes, '[it] was partially responsible for perpetuating, or indeed widening, the gulf between vocational courses and liberal studies' that was to plague British adult education for the rest of the century and beyond (see Fieldhouse, 1996: 48).

The departure of the Hibberts to Ackworth and Maurice Rowntree's retirement from the scene created a period of uncertainty for Swarthmore. Edmund Harvey, whose father William Harvey had been one of the principal funders, stepped into the breach although it was clear his political ambitions meant he would not stay in post for long. Despite leaving to stand as Liberal candidate for Dewsbury the following year, he maintained a near life-long involvement with Swarthmore – mostly as President of the Council – and discrete benefactor. Since he was married to Arnold Rowntree's sister, it was still in many ways a family concern. Although it retained its core commitment to religious study and social reform, during the 1920s Swarthmore changed in character. It lost some of its wartime radicalism and became more eclectic. It broadened its appeal from the original Quaker and Adult School leaders and welcomed all those who genuinely wished to learn more about the world but, crucially, wanted to enjoy its gifts. Reports note the 'variety of vocations of life' that meets at Swarthmore and the youthfulness of students 'mostly in the full vigour of life'. Richard Swain's 'breezy personality and youthful enthusiasm' inspired all and complemented Hodgson's quieter style.

## The Student Guild and a Student Democracy

But 12 Clarendon Rd was now too small and Swarthmore moved down the hill to new premises that had become available at 4 Woodhouse Square. Even so, No. 4 was 'not ideal' and there was considerable concern about finances. One of the most important functional changes was the formation of the Students' Guild in 1920 with 125 members, which shifted the balance of determination of the Settlement distinctly towards the students, who had hitherto no say in the running of the centre. The Guild formed debating, choral and play-reading societies and took over organising the rambles and, for the first time, cooperated in nominating members of Council – there were no elections at this stage. 'New forces were at work', bringing a democratic vitality to the centre. Led by Miss Amy Harrison as President, they cleaned, renovated and furnished the new premises and created a tradition of Saturday evening socials. Stimulated by the *1919 Report's* emphasis on democratic control, Swarthmore's much vaunted voluntarism really dates from this period. Generally the Students' Guild built up a much fuller social life for members, especially through the Play Reading Society developed from 1924.

Hodgson became Warden in 1921 but tragically Swain died in the summer, a report noting that he 'leaves many a life brighter and better' and a spark appeared to have gone out. Swarthmore too was no longer simply an independent centre

**Charles E. Hodgson, PhD**

Warden: 1921-27,
Sub Warden 1920.
A scholarly man, at first sight appears to have lacked the fire-in-the-belly of his predecessors. Maybe he was not the evangelical missionary but he nurtured the Settlement and its students and presided over the beginnings of sustained growth that continued for two decades. In the 1949 report, for example, Edmund Harvey wrote that he was a 'gentle spirit', unassuming, keen and kind. He 'discovered people who had lost their attachment to churches and other communities and provided them with a new community where the Settlement became central, a spiritual home' (Harvey, 1949).

and entered the process in which ultimately it becomes a part, though a very independently minded part, of the state system of education. Under the recommendation of the *1919 Report*, classes were recognised for the first time for a Board of Education grant administered through Leeds Local Education Authority. Courses that were 'recognised' received £10 per session but not the less formal classes such as Bible study and religious history. This gave the Settlement greater financial security though to the far sighted it became clear that its provision might at some stage have to be tailored to the funder's calling.

The centre grew remarkably – the staff doubled to 8 and classes trebled to 21 by 1927. Its increasingly international spirit was shown when receipts for performances of a play by Tolstoy, performed at Swarthmore, were sent to the Russian famine relief fund in 1921 (caused by the Civil War). Swarthmore's own 'extension' work was flourishing. Despite his political activities, Edmund Harvey found the time to begin classes in Armley Gaol for Juvenile Adults beginning in April 1921, a provision which is eventually taken over by the WEA and lasted through to the 1980s. The three university students still in residence helped out and sympathetic Leeds University lecturers became increasingly involved.

Gradually Swarthmore started to expand and despite Hodgson's low key approach, the Students' Guild injected a dynamism into the Settlement which first appeared as a heightened social life and then made its mark on the curriculum. The syllabus now offered around 20 courses per week and student numbers steadily grew over the 200 mark. New subjects began to appear on the syllabus such as Appreciation of Art, taught by a team of tutors and Psychology, taught by Hodgson himself, as well as courses on the American Colonies, German Language and culture and English Literature. For the first time there was a class on Mathematics, which had been asked for by the members of the Student's Guild. New tutors, who soon become part of the fabric of the Settlement, established themselves. Jean P. Inebnit, for example, taught no less than three French classes, from beginners to advanced, to which he brought a cultivated, pacifist sensibility.

## Swarthmore Settlement.

Founded 1909

4, Woodhouse Square, Clarendon Rd., Leeds.

### Syllabus FOR THE Spring Term,

January 14th to March 27th, 1926.

Teaching Staff—
C. E. HODGSON, M.A., Ph.D. (Warden)
J. W. MANN.    Miss M. E. JAGGER, M.Sc.
J. P. INEBNIT.    F. DEAN.
G. P. MEREDITH, B.Sc.   A. FREEMAN, M.A.
Miss M. M. SCOTT.    S. TODD,
Mrs. M. G. FEATHERSTONE, M.A.

*Front cover and inside pages from the 1926 Swarthmore Settlement Spring Syllabus of lectures*

### Mondays — Commencing JANUARY 18th.

- 7-0 ... ELEMENTARY GERMAN — C. E. Hodgson
- 7-0 ... COUNTRY DANCING — M. M. Scott
- 8-0 ... ENGLISH SOCIAL HISTORY — C. E. Hodgson
- 8-0 ... MATHEMATICS — G. P. Meredith
- 8-0 ... BOTANY — M. E. Jagger

### Tuesdays — Commencing JANUARY 19th.

- 3-0 ... THE WORLD ABOUT US (For details see separate cards).
- 7-0 ... ELEMENTARY ESPERANTO — J. W. Mann
- 7-0 ... ADULT SCHOOL LEADERS' PREPARATION CLASS — C. E. Hodgson
- 7-0 ... ELEMENTARY FRENCH — J. P. Inebnit
- 8-0 ... ADVANCED ESPERANTO — J. W. Mann
- 8-0 ... STUDIES IN RELIGION — C. E. Hodgson
- 8-0 ... PLAY-READING and DEBATING SOCIETIES ALTERNATELY

### Wednesdays — Commencing JANUARY 20th.

- 7-45 ... OXFORD UNIVERSITY TUTORIAL CLASS (Industrial History of the 19th Century) — A. Freeman
- 8-0 ... LOGIC—METHODS OF REASONING — C. E. Hodgson

### Thursdays — Commencing JANUARY 21st.

- 7-0 ... GERMAN TRANSLATION and COMPOSITION — S. Todd
- 7-30 ... SKETCHING CLASS — F. Dean
- 7-30 ... FIRST AID (Ladies) — L. Capper Johnson
- 8-0 ... PROBLEMS OF SUPPLY IN INDUSTRY — M. G. Featherstone
- 8-0 ... GERMAN TRANSLATION and CONVERSATION — S. Todd

### Fridays — Commencing JANUARY 22nd.

- 7-0 ... FRENCH GRAMMAR and COMPOSITION — J. P. Inebnit
- 7-0 ... ENGLISH GRAMMAR and COMPOSITION — C. E. Hodgson
- 8-0 ... FRENCH HISTORY and LITERATURE — J. P. Inebnit
- 8-0 ... ENGLISH LITERATURE: MODERN WRITERS — C. E. Hodgson

### Saturdays — Commencing JANUARY 23rd.

- 7-0 ... SPECIAL SERIES OF LECTURES (for details of which see separate cards).

The STUDENTS' GUILD SOCIALS will be held on the first Saturday of each month, on which evenings there will be no lectures.

The Sunday FELLOWSHIP MEETING will be held on the first Sunday in each month, at 6-30 p.m.

### Jean Inebnit (1890-1982)

Although originally a Swiss national, he was imprisoned as a conscientious objector in WWI. He spent over 50 years in England and taught at Leeds University. He joined the Friends in London in 1920 and became a major figure in British Quakerism. A member of LYM "Meeting for Sufferings", he was a founder member of the International Volunteers for Peace (IVSP) and ran work camps which brought many English Quakers and potential Swiss Quakers together.

### English Quakers and potential Swiss Quakers together

Inebnit's French classes deepened Swarthmore's commitment to language teaching in the context of a growing interest in European culture, complementing Hodgson's German classes. The international language, Esperanto, was taught for the first time by J. W. Mann and remained on the syllabus for many years.

Although with Swain's death the science courses declined somewhat, a course in botany was still offered and one in astronomy (with lantern illustrations) taught by R. Stonely. This may be something of a joke in Leeds where, thanks to the prodigious smoke of industrial and domestic chimneys, the sky at night was rarely visible. (It was not the first time astronomy had been taught in evening classes. The first was for the Leeds Ladies Educational Association during the 1870s, when it was provided by the University of Cambridge Extension Committee. The irony was that the women had asked for resources to support a teacher training programme but got astronomy instead (Swindells, 1995: 43)). Stonely followed up with a special lecture on Neighbouring Worlds. By the mid 1920s a further change of style was marked by classes on Country Dancing, the Art of Music, Play-reading and Sketching, indicating a drift towards the leisure and practical arts and away from the rigours of Bible study. Hodgson nevertheless still offered classes for Adult School leaders and one on the New Testament, for the first time since the war, complemented by classes in Ethics and Logic. But almost half the programme was taken up by language teaching, now well arranged in a progressive sequence from beginners to advanced and including composition.

With the syllabus becoming more responsive to student demand, there was a distinct feeling of a loosening of the reins. This was reflected in the statement on the programme, which now maintained that:

> *The Settlement aims to provide opportunities for higher education and to increase the equipment of religious and social workers. It is open to all who desire to learn without distinction of religious or political views.*

By comparison with the call to public service of Swarthmore's 1915 statement, which noted that the Settlement: 'is open to all who desire to study the problems of to-day, and to equip themselves for the better service of humanity', this lacks urgency. Nevertheless, the treatment of social and political affairs was obvious in classes on English and French History, Problems of Supply in Industry and The Governance of the City and the World About Us, for example. A class on International Problems invited members to consider the League of Nations idea and the Oxford Tutorial Class on the State and Industry, although no longer taken by Henry Clay, remained popular. The Settlement's outreach work included a 'tutorial' economics class in Rawdon given by a former Swarthmore student.

However, the increasing role of the Student Guild offered a different sort of emphasis which was more about sociability, self-expression and artistic enjoyment. Here the spontaneous self-organising abilities of the members were encouraged and became the seeds for something of an artistic renaissance in an otherwise quite puritan environment. Two plays were performed and the Guild organised lectures on Palestine and Gandhi by Kastiri Raj jointly with the WEA. It continued to promote fellowship through rambles. Through the Guild's expansion of its social life and increasingly involvement in the curriculum, Swarthmore was beginning to look like a student democracy but it was not there yet.

While Hodgson had presided over a modest increase in student numbers to about 230 and a broadening out of Swarthmore's activities, certain important changes in atmosphere had taken place. He slipped away in 1927 almost as quietly as he had arrived six years earlier – characteristically, one of his last contributions was a special lecture on 'a Holiday in Northern France'. He was thanked for his 'never failing sympathy, tact and patience' in the following Annual Report – but there was no mention of the Strike.

## Wilfred Allott and the 'International Idea'

With Allott's arrival in 1927 a dramatic shift took place and there was something of a return to the spirit of the founding years. But in other respects the changes that had begun after WWI were, if anything, encouraged. Although the deaths of two of the founders, William Harvey and William Whiting,

## Wilfrid Allott, 1891-1972

Warden: 1927-43. One of the original students lodging at 12 Clarendon Rd with Gerald Hibbert who regarded him as 'one of my spiritual sons' (Hibbert, 1949). He remained as Warden for sixteen years and by the outbreak of WW2 in 1939, student membership had tripled to over 700 while 1938 was a record year for classes, 52 in number. Became a very influential figure in modern Quakerism, lecturing widely and writing frequently - gave 1945 Swarthmore (USA) Lecture on Worship and Social Progress. Told the ESA council in 1936 that 'history, art, science and languages should lie at the heart of a settlement's curriculum, and that the last of these should include English grammar' (Freeman 2004: 129-30).

who had put considerable sums both of energy and money into Swarthmore, caused considerable grief, the move away from their original vision of a Bible-centred learning for AS leaders continued apace and a new student body had taken shape. During this period the social dynamic being established by the Student Guild developed strongly and Swarthmore gradually became more substantially equipped both for teaching and socialising, with an enlarged library, newspapers, and even carpets, all foraged for by the enthusiastic volunteers of the Guild. The programme of classes expanded further into arts and crafts and even courses on the 'Mysteries of the Universe', the class membership rising quickly. Allott, however, did not entirely abandon the Bible studies and indeed introduced the first New Testament class to be taught in over ten years but his genius was to grasp the nature of the change and make it into a serious new project.

This was 'Internationalism'. Already implicit in the expansion of classes into languages during Hodgson's years, Allott made it into a cause. He frequently alluded to it in his annual reports: 'By our language classes we keep alive and inform the International idea' he wrote in 1930 and in other places insisted the true function of language teaching was to gain an understanding of and empathy with the people of other countries. He insisted, 'Our work in foreign languages is cultural in aim'. Although it would be true to say that the intention was truly global internationalism, in practice the focus was on Europe and uniting it in the face of the rise of totalitarian threats. With some foresight, he quoted the great Italian philosopher Bernadetto Croce on the need for a European union in which 'men's hearts will beat for Europe as they once did for their smaller countries'. Allott himself offered a course on the Growth of International Thought, based on F. W. Stawell's *History of International Thought*. This was a study in the thought and historical setting of figures who had promoted international understanding in the context of a common humanity, such as Augustine, Dante, Erasmus and Rousseau. International Relations remained a standard element of the programme, inevitably focusing on the rise of fascism throughout the period. A course on the Great Powers even included a passionate contribution from a supporter of Hitler called Heinrich Lamprecht who, in true Swarthmore fashion, was politely heard out and then challenged intensively in debate.

As we shall see this new internationalism opened the door for a remarkable change in Swarthmore's membership, when during the 1930s waves of European immigrants, often Jewish, escaping Nazi persecution, arrived in Leeds. Swarthmore offered a warm welcome for these displaced groups and took on a remarkable cosmopolitan ambience. Jean Inebnit had already established teaching in French language and history and German was well established but the arrival of new tutor in 1929 took it to new heights. This was Martha Steinitz. She immediately offered four classes in German and in the (perhaps not so well chosen) words of Allott 'took no prisoners'. When Allott assumed the Wardenship in 1927 language teaching occupied something like 40% of the programme and by 1940 had risen to 50%. So languages became the bedrock of Swarthmore provision.

By the end of the 1930s Allott was offering courses on English for Foreigners for the new wave of dispossessed refugees and immigrants. These were complemented by more literature classes, teaching many of them himself and slanting them to a certain extent towards writing and self-expression. In 1938–39 for example the object of his literature course was to examine how the best modern writers actually work, taking examples from E.M. Forster's *Passage to India* and the poems of Robert Graves and Wilfrid Owen.

## The New Curriculum

But what about the rest of the programme? This was split into two major themes: the 'serious' social science subjects offered by the WEA and the university, while the arts and crafts and play reading programme, stimulated by the Students' Guild, were Swarthmore's own, sponsored by the ESA. The partnership with the WEA had been revived by the return from New Zealand, after a six year absence, of George Thompson as District Secretary. He replaced Ernest Green who in turn had left to become the WEA National Secretary in London (much to the relief of the WEA's Yorkshire pioneers). Thompson also 'took no prisoners' and re-established the serious three year Tutorial Class programme in social sciences and music. By the late 1930s 'WEA' tutorials, as they were known, included Economics, Geography: the geographical basis of world problems, two music classes by Edward Pybus, Social Philosophy taken by Prof. H.C. Rowse and Political Theory by

### Martha Steinitz

Born 11 Mar 1889, Kattowitz, Germany/ Poland, died 24 May 1966, Leeds.

Martha was the youngest of ten children; her mother was 41 when she was born just five years before her father's death at the age of 56. Edith Jones (daughter of William Whiting) in a letter to Swarthmore of 5 Dec 1966 claims that she was one of a group of German women invited to spend Xmas with the Whiting family in 1921, who decided to stay. She was a peace activist and led a Disarmament study group on Sunday evenings. Another letter from Winifred Booth (nee Barnes) of 18 Nov 1966, says she was instrumental in placing an Austrian refugee girl with her.

Members of her class reminisced about the commitment she expected, one noting how her troubled friend had gone to Steinitz for sympathy about the difficulty of the vocabulary she had to learn and getting the response, 'Well, do you want to learn German or not?' Steinitz not only took on a substantial teaching load for the next thirty years but assiduously translated German classics – particularly those of her hero Goethe – but she also wrote plays especially for her advanced group to perform. Some of these were in fact published and the reputation she began to achieve as a German scholar, including praise from Thomas Mann for her adaptation of his novel 'Buddenbrooks', led Leeds University to offer her an honorary MA in 1961.

Frank McCulloch. Rowse, who became a long-term stalwart of Swarthmore, initiated the study of psychology and his colleague, James Irving, offered a Tutorial Class on Psychology and Politics on the same programme in 1938–39. This was at a time when the idea of the 'mass psychology' of fascism was under urgent scrutiny. Allott taught a class on history which centred on social and political life in Europe, and another looking at the church's influenced on education, moral standards and peace up to 'the conflict with modern dictatorships'. The theme of the immanent threat of fascism was continued in a subsequent course centred on the 'change in the public spirit of Europe in recent years and the clash of ideals and interests today'. In the summer too there were serious studies of contemporary ideas such as Prof. Rowse's course on Philosophies of our Time that considered the work of Bergson, Lytton Strachey and Aldous Huxley, which attracted 40 students.

The last of the Oxford Tutorial Classes that had begun with Henry Clay in 1910, was one taught by Dr Lance Jones in Political Theory, 1931–32. It too was a great success, the report from the class secretary reproduced in the 1932 Annual Report concluding:

> *The session was devoted chiefly to an examination of the machinery of politics, the basis of the state, the judiciaries system, sovereignty, right etc., with a cogence at the newer manifestations of politics, the progressive changes in the collectivist proposals for state socialism through syndicalism to guilds and sovietism, winding up by a comparison of the soviet and fascist dictatorships...ingeniously illustrated by the tutor by means of excerpts from students' essays which were thus subjected to class discussion'.*

It seems to have been a perfect blend of informed comment and democratic discussion. A year or so later the class was taken over by Frank McCulloch, a hugely popular tutor, and brought into the WEA/Leeds University Joint Committee programme. This ended Swarthmore's twenty year association with Oxford and was a cause of concern among older members. The reason was that the Leeds University Joint Committee (which, jointly with the WEA, organised the Tutorial Classes programme) was always a matter of controversy while George Thompson was the committee's secretary. Although the programme was nominally in the university's gift, there was no doubt about who actually ran it. Since at this time Leeds University lacked a Department of Extra Mural Studies, the five full-time staff tutors (of whom McCulloch was one) were paid through the Joint Committee – which suited Thompson very well since he became their de-facto employer. To illustrate the view of Thompson taken by his 'employees', a story goes that McCulloch had been loaned a copy of Hitler's *Mein Kampf* by his colleague Sidney Raybould. On returning it, McCulloch's comment was that Hitler was indeed small fry compared with George Thompson (letter to Raybould 1938, See Steele, 1989). Much to Thompson's dismay, Raybould became the first Director of the University's Extra-Mural Department when it was founded in 1946.

While the three-year tutorial was Thompson's favoured instrument of education, the WEA offered one-year classes in various aspects of science, politics and society. Joe Belton's course on This Mysterious Universe for example, was in fact an attempt to 'explain the latest scientific theory of the nature of things'. The scientific strand was further promoted by Allott's wife in a course on the Science of Life which drew on H.G. Wells's book of he same name. Occasionally botany appeared on the programme but it was changing subtly. Mrs Allott for example offered a course on Plants and Human Economics, which has a remarkably contemporary ecological feel. It inquired into the principles of botany and how plants made it possible to assimilate non-living materials, studying inheritance, plant breeding and hybrids.

A radical new departure in group study was provided by the BBC from 1932 when it offered Group-Listening programmes. Swarthmore turned these into study groups at the Settlement with former students acting as group leaders. Stimulation if any was necessary, came from the fact that the first of the BBC's study programmes was made by no less than Henry Clay on Industry and Economics, Allott reminding members that in Swarthmore's early years, Clay had taught there in person. Other programmes in the series included Eustace Percy, Leonard Woolf and others on the Last Thirty Years and John Dover Wilson, now a celebrated Shakespeare critic, on Education. Some WEA members would have remembered him as the enthusiastic young HMI who would occasionally sit in on classes around WWI. In this role Wilson had kept an official eye on the formation the Yorkshire District of the WEA in 1914 in what in national circles was regarded as a rather dangerous move (since it was a vehemently opposed rupture from the WEA's Northern District). Reflecting some fourteen years later, he declared the Yorkshire District was something exceptional: the 'greatest instrument for the development of adult education that this country had yet seen' (Dover Wilson, 1928: 49: quoted in Steele, 1987: 111). This was in large part, he believed, because of the qualities displayed by its founding district secretary G. H. Thompson, whose puritan insistence on the rigours of the three year tutorial class and devotion to the working-class movement, made the Yorkshire District almost unique in its dedication to educational seriousness and social purpose (Harrison 1961: 289–299). He was not at all dismayed by Thompson's insistence on the centrality of what he called the 'controversial' subjects of politics, economics, social history and theory, because he believed this reflected the genuine needs of the movement and that the arts and humanities would follow in due time. Not all Swarthmore members were so sanguine.

New subjects emerging from the ethos of the Students' Guild that became regulars on the programme included two classes in Folk Dancing led by Miss Spence with Miss Bramley on piano and Arts and Crafts, the early steps in the impressively creative programme Swarthmore was to offer by the 1960s. These focused on leather, cane and rush, raffia and pewter work 'according to choice' taught by Miss K Noble. The play-reading and debating societies initially met alternately on Tuesdays. Play-reading and performance were to become mainstreamed classes by the mid-1930s when they begin to appear under the 'English' section of the programme with readings on Tuesday nights and rehearsals on Fridays – in one year attempting no less than seventeen plays. Although many of these are of their time and now long-forgotten a substantial number of serious modern plays included: O'Casey's *Juno and the Paycock,* Pirandello's *Six Characters in Search of an Author,* Auden and Isherwood's *On the Frontier* and *The Ascent of F6,* O'Neill's *Mourning becomes Electra* and T. S. Eliot's *Family Reunion.*

Swarthmore had, under Allott's stewardship, therefore moved a long way from the educational provision of its founding fathers. Yet in key aspects the vision was very much the same, as revealed in an interesting declaration on the reverse of the 1933–34 syllabus. This claimed that adult education:

> *is based on the adequate experience of grown men and women; it abandons therefore the schoolmaster's authority and the Specialist University Course and works by free discussion of matter of the student's choice, its immediate object is fellowship in living intellectual and social interests.*

Allott had in effect creatively responded to the needs of the times and especially the transition from a paternalistic Quaker organisation to something resembling a popular student democracy. Although the change in the constitution that would confirm this by allowing direct elections to the Council was a few years off, in many respects the curriculum and conduct of classes already reflected student preferences. The warden's role was to respect this while at the same time maintaining the founding ideals.

## Change and Continuity

But how had Swarthmore changed as an educational organisation? Firstly although it had begun to receive larger grants from the LEA, its finances were substantially on the same basis as before. With the deaths of it founders William Whiting and William Harvey, Swarthmore had long since metamorphosed from being purely a 'place for Friends'. Elements of the Quaker family firm remained, however, as Edmund Harvey still actively occupied the Chairmanship of the Council and Edwin Rowntree held the keys to its treasury. To take the year 1938, the Settlement's most successful year to date, the income received was £1097 – almost double the founding sum of £600 in 1909, almost thirty years earlier, but still a very modest sum. Quaker benefactors still contributed but to a much lesser extent; the Leeds Friends Trust, for example, gave only £25, the Sir James Reckitt Charity, £30 and the Woodhead Trust donated £105. By far the largest amount, £350, came from the Educational Settlements Association (ESA), the national body linking settlements like Swarthmore and Fircroft, which had been set up in 1929 by Swarthmore's own patrons, Edmund Harvey and Ernest Taylor. An extra £48 was received in individual donations. Remarkably, student fees contributed almost a third at £311 but the most significant new source of funds was Leeds Education Authority which contributed £180 (on the basis of £10 for each course that fitted its educational criteria). So charitable funding amounted to around half the revenue, student fees one third and Leeds C.C. about a sixth. In terms of expenditure, two thirds, £698, went in salaries and the rest on rent, rates and running the show. Ten years later, after WW2, these proportions were to look very different but by then everything had changed.

## Membership

How had the membership changed? As we have noted 1937–38 (the 29th year) was a record year, offering 52 classes in all. Student numbers had climbed to 744 in the winter and 486 in the summer, making 1230 in all or roughly six times the original student membership in 1909–10. Very few of these now participated in Adult Schools as leaders but according the to the annual report they were still 'as serious as the times demand' and a solid core still attended tutorial classes in the social sciences. A special course on World Affairs, suggested by the students' committee had attracted 99 students, for example. There had of course been a spectacular rise in language classes, including 15 in French and German, or a little over a third of the provision. The number of students in German courses had risen from 101 in 1933–34 to 244 in 1937–38 'despite the Hitler regime', it was claimed. The cause of Internationalism or Europeanism had in many respects replaced the original appeal to West Riding missionary work and this was reflected by an influx of foreign refugees, for whom Swarthmore had become a kind of spiritual home. A further new group of students, mostly women, were attracted by the growing Arts and Crafts programme, while would-be actors from miles around joined the play-reading classes. This reflected the intense interest in amateur dramatics and play-going in Leeds, which had a number of theatre groups and clubs including a Jewish Theatre group and Jacob Kramer's infamous Eyebrow Club (a pun on 'highbrow' but also because their productions raised an eyebrow – they performed only plays banned by the censor including, on one celebrated occasion, *Salome* by Oscar Wilde). A Leeds Unity Theatre, performing plays with a strong socialist content, was formed by Alex Baron in 1939.

Swarthmore thus tried to balance the needs of serious study, international understanding, recreation and personal expression in an atmosphere of friendship and tolerance. This diversity prompted from Allot a reflection on why people came to Swarthmore:

> *The majority come in the first instance to study a particular subject; a number come because their schooling ended so early that it fails even as a start in the social and political world. Some people look for a leisure pursuit as a contrast to their work …A man from home comes for friendship and becomes interested in classes. A small minority come to equip themselves for service of one kind or another. Very few come for vocational training; it is recognised that this is not our job.*
> (1937–38 Annual Report)

### Above all, 'not for vocational training'

In the 1931–32 report Allott had quoted from Aristotle on the need for education – now an 'emergency policy' for 'evil times'. He had noted that the ESA movement had contributed to making 'thinking and well informed adults' but they were still a 'dangerously small' minority. His occupational survey of membership revealed that about 35% were in white collar jobs, 30% were manual labourers, and there were 15% teachers and a further 10% who were engaged in 'household duties' (i.e. housewives). It does not mention gender balance but probably at this time it was about equal with a preponderance of men in social science classes and women in Arts and Crafts. By the end of WW2, as we shall see, this balance was to shift decisively in favour of women contemporaneously with a sharp decline in social science. Always concerned about the relative absence of manual workers, it was regularly debated in on the Council and various schemes of outreach work proposed, but the balance remained resolutely the same.

Another fruitful result of Swarthmore's open door policy was the number of other associations that contributed to it including not only the WEA but the campaign group No More War and the Holiday Fellowship. The very active role of the Student Committee (which had changed its name from 'Student Guild' in about 1930) was obvious in the reports.

Frank Dodd, its secretary, had even on occasion co-signed the report with Allott and one summer when the Warden was away at Woodbrooke (where his mentor Gerald Hibbert was reviving the case of religious education), had managed the entire summer programme. Representatives were sent to the ESA annual conference as well as organising rambles, social weekends, the library, the canteen and housekeeping. The committee, it is fair to say, changed the look of Swarthmore. It organised volunteers to do the painting and decoration, gathered second hand furniture and carpets, created the canteen, supervised the library and found it books. Its voluntarism was another key to Swarthmore's distinction as an educational centre. Lastly, certain individuals played an essential role. The 'wise and inspiring' influence of Martha Steinitz, was first noted in 1929 and by 1934 she was teaching four German courses and one on Art Appreciation weekly. She was a prolific writer and published plays some of which were enacted by the Swarthmore Players. Steinitz seemed responsible for welcoming the swathes of displaced European (especially Jewish) refugees, through Swarthmore's doors, getting them to learn English and tell their stories.

The growing economic depression and consequent unemployment of the 1930s saw Swarthmore waiving its fees for unemployed workers. The alarming events on mainland Europe, where the advance of fascism had already been felt in the number of refugees arriving in Leeds, raised concerns about the future of civilisation and lectures, for example, on the Failure of Liberalism in Germany by Prof. John Harvey, Edmund's brother, were popular. The adventurous spirit of the members that had found rambling groups visiting Germany for a tour of the Rhine in 1929 (of which a pictorial log book still exists, though not unfortunately a written one) gave way to urgent speculation, an enrolment of 144 in the class on World Affairs alone.

Only towards the end of his period as Warden in 1936, did Allott feel able to sum up what he felt were the essential bases of learning in a Settlement like Swarthmore:

> *History ought in one way or another to be the centre of the Settlement curriculum. There was a danger to-day in the doctrine of fresh starts, but history showed that there was nothing very fresh. Moreover the study of history led*

*people away from lesser loyalties to a sense of universal humanity, often attracting pity and always reverence. Next to history came art, which became absolutely vital in middle life. It provided an outlet through poetry, painting the drama and music by which people could get outside themselves and be absorbed in apparently infinite beauty. The third subject was science. Everyone should do some science or other. Economics was the most important. No settlement could afford to neglect discussing such vital subjects as international law. It was just as important to educate the citizens of to-day as the child – perhaps more important since many of the social sciences were not considered suitable for children still at school. Lastly there was the important subject of language.*
(quoted in Freeman, 2004: 130)

The years had taken a toll on Allott's health and shortly into the War he was forced to take a break but he had successfully transformed Swarthmore into a lively but more secular student democracy.

## CHAPTER 4

# War, Reconstruction and Revival, 1939–1960

1938 was the golden year. Swarthmore vibrated with life, purpose and diversity, but then came Munich and Neville Chamberlain's appeasement of the Nazi threat. His 'piece of paper' only bought time for Hitler to prepare his assault on Europe and the Soviet Union and once again rumours of war and then the thing itself took charge. Membership plummeted to just over 400 and then 330 in 1940–41 and total fees fell to £162. During the following winter Swarthmore even closed, unprecedentedly, for two of the worst winter months. Many of its stalwarts were enlisted or joined voluntarily and many pacifists volunteered for ambulance service or other occupations. The strain took its toll on Allott who was granted a year's sabbatical leave in 1942 and Stanley Thompson his deputy took over as Warden for a year, but Allott did not return. Thompson also retired and returned to China to continue his missionary work. Swarthmore thus had a rocky ride through the opening of the war and even the annual report for 1939–1940 was held over. Blackouts, paper shortage, food rationing, the loss of both men and women to war service (vivid accounts of which survive in the log book that Allott started at the beginning of the war, which was completed by other members) threatened its very existence.

But just when it seemed that Swarthmore's fortunes were irreversibly sinking, it bounced back. A new relationship with the Army saw its numbers swelling by over 190, with service men and, particularly, women from the Army Pay Corps stationed in Leeds. Swarthmore which had been so welcoming to European refugees before the war now became khaki-clad. While special English for Refugees classes grew, practical courses like First Aid and Nursing attracted over 100 enrolments and by 1942 numbers had again risen to record heights (568 in the winter). An Ulsterman, Desmond Neill, whose experience at St Mary's in York was invaluable, was appointed Warden in 1943. However, the frequent – but largely unnecessary – alarms of the air-raid sirens meant that the newly built shelter had regularly to be utilised as an emergency classroom. This was not always to the mutual convenience of classes, especially when the drama group had previously claimed it for rehearsals and thespian declaiming drowned out quiet discussion. Bad for the ears maybe, but walking home in the blackout carried even greater risks.

Not surprisingly perhaps, Swarthmore's rambling and cycling clubs flourished as members were only too keen to escape the gloom of war-weary Leeds (despite receiving little attention from German bombers), their log books testifying to healthy pursuits in the countryside, so long as you watched where you were putting your feet when walking over army training grounds littered with unexploded shells and bombs. The rambles seemed to bring out the poetic, as this extract from a 1942 log entry shows:

> *Having donned boots and collected our packed lunches, we decided to make our way to Gordale Scar. It was a morning to make you feel 'on top of the world'. The air was crisp, the sun beamed upon us, and everywhere was light covering of snow. Soon we were gazing in awe at the Scar, clothed in her winter garb. The waterfall was still cascading over the rocks, but long icicles hung in weird and wonderful shapes. As the sun caught them, they glistened brightly and clearly, sending pencils of silver light into the deep recesses of nearby rocks. Away over our heads was a balcony of rocks so heavily and intricately fringed with a network of icicles, that it looked as if Jack Frost had been preparing for the appearance of royalty. We stared at this superb artistry, and reluctantly retraced our steps to the road, and tried to reconcile all to the fact that we had entered the fourth year of the war.*
> (Log Book 1942–44, entry by Freddy Glover,: 59)

But, however distantly, the end was in sight and a rising tide of interest in courses and pressure on premises to accommodate the coming peace manifested itself. Membership rose again in 1943–44 to 712, another record, though dropping slightly in 1944–45 to 685 (not including members of the forces who attended classes without payment, of whom there were 164 in 1944–45, most of whom were women). In gender terms an

**Desmond Neill**

Warden 1943–1946. Previously served at Swarthmore's sister educational settlement St Mary's in York. A social scientist by training, he also left in 1946 to become Director of the Social Sciences Dept at Queens University, Belfast, where he pioneered the development of what was then a relatively infant academic subject in British universities.

interesting shift had taken place, women now outrunning men by almost 4 to1. Languages were still the most popular subject group, accounting for almost half of all classes – 22 in all and stimulated by the Pay Corps demands – followed by social sciences (mostly WEA and tutorial) and literature and arts. An occupational survey of members in 1944-45 revealed, to much disappointment, that only about 10% (71) were manual workers, while white collar workers represented nearly half (314) and professionals around 30% (195) of whom teachers were 108 or nearly half. It was still felt there was a 'solid group' for social sciences and The Whither Democracy? lectures in the summer attracted 60-70 students. Drama flourished under a new leader, Edith Whitaker, but the musical recitals faltered and were reluctantly ended.

Swarthmore members at the Holiday Fellowship Guest House, 1941

However, a good attendance at showings of documentary films provided by the Ministry of Information, suggested a new subject for the syllabus, Film Studies, as we shall see. Students also envied the facilities provided at the folk high schools in Sweden, as described in a talk by Nils Bosson, Rektor of Tarna Folk High School. The Students committee was still very active in organising socials, rambles and cycling tours and the log book was revitalised by Mrs Glover's editorship, while the library was re-catalogued and expanded.

## The Social Studies and Reconstruction

Despite the disruption, Swarthmore's provision of classes during the war was still of a remarkably high quality. There was a large social science and humanities programme that included two tutorial classes on Philosophy, one by John Harvey the brother of Edmund who was a Professor of Philosophy at Leeds (1932-1954) and who was now Chair of Swarthmore Council. The other was by James Cameron later also to become Professor of Philosophy and head of department. A third philosophy class was given by the remarkable Harry Guntrip on Psychology and Philosophy. His course related the major philosophical theories of Plato, Aristotle, Kant, Hegel and Marx to the psychoanalytical theories of Freud, Adler and Jung and attempted to outline a philosophy for everyday life. Guntrip went on to lead the influential School of Psychiatry at Leeds and was responsible for profound changes in the subject. A Congregational minister at Salem church and practising psychotherapist, he was heavily influenced by the personal relationship philosophy of the Scottish philosopher John MacMurray and Martin Büber; which he applied to his psychoanalytic work. His Oxford DNB entry notes that:

> [H]e strove to integrate religion and psychoanalysis, seeing both of them as dedicated vocations to bring God's love and understanding... Guntrip's writings have been influential and have made psychoanalysis, in particular object relations theory, more accessible. They are the writings of a man with a mission to communicate and to convert, and represent his own integration of religion and psychodynamic science.

Guntrip also contributed to the series of discussions on Whither Democracy? in 1944 which also included talks by Harvey and Prof Bonamy Dobree on the Role of an Author in a

Developed Democracy. Dobree, (who was incidentally Richard Hoggart's academic mentor when Hoggart was an undergraduate at Leeds) was a highly influential academic reformer, responsible for creating the Gregory Fellowships and founding the Department of Fine Art at Leeds University. It was also consistent with Swarthmore's tradition of unflinching pluralism that platforms were offered to the main political parties including the Communist Party. A further series on Aspects of Reconstruction also included the charismatic chairman of Leeds City Council's Housing Committee, Rev. C. Jenkinson.

The Warden, Desmond Neill, also offered courses in the social sciences including one on the Problems of Economic Planning and one on The American Way, studying how social and political institutions related to economic structures. A third, on Contemporary Social Doctrines, studied the ideas of and backgrounds to fascism, communism, democracy and Catholic social thought. There were further courses on International Relations and Town and Country Planning but perhaps the most remarkable were a series of classes on the Jewish People given by Martha Steinitz. She looked squarely at the problems of anti-Semitism, the history of Judaism and the consequences of Jewish immigration to Britain and Leeds especially. One course, which was a joint investigation, was even called the Jew and his Neighbour. A further course on the Jew in the Modern World focused on the rise of Zionism and, prophetically, the problem of Palestine. Steinitz, who never took less than five German language courses during the 1940s, also offered in 1946 what may have been the precursor to 'second wave feminism' at Swarthmore. This was Great Women of Our Time, which studied the contribution made by women politicians, social reformers, educationists, writers and artists to modern civilisation that included the educators, Maria Montessori, Margaret Macmillan and Jane Addams, the political reformer, Beatrice Webb and Martha Steinitz's revolutionary compatriot, Rosa Luxembourg.

In June 1943 the BBC visited Swarthmore to stage a discussion concerned with the 'The Four Freedoms and Social Security'; the story is taken up by T. W. Metcalf in the pages of the Wartime Log Book, illustrating the earnestness of Swarthmore's students but also their willingness to listen and learn:

*Stimulated by this interesting title, eight worthy students armed with notebooks and wearing expressions of grim determination proceeded to put forward their views for a better world. The gentleman from the BBC soon realised that he had got quite a mixed bag, for the view put forward ranged from the pessimistic and cynical to optimistic and ultra scarlet Communistic. The group had no difficulty in deciding what was wrong with our present mode of life, but when we tried to find the solution to the many problems, we were soon faced with complexity.* (Log Book 1942–45: 85)

Cycle run to Eavestone Lake
North Yorkshire, 1945

The Literature Drama and Art programme also expanded in novel ways. The Play-Reading group studied no less than 20 plays by Shakespeare, Chekhov, Shaw and Ibsen, and performed some one-acters at socials. Specialists were also invited in to give classes on stagecraft and management and the celebrated Shakespearian critic and editor, Kenneth Muir, then at Leeds University also lectured on Types of English Drama, making Swarthmore one of the most serious centres for the study of drama in Yorkshire. A new addition to the syllabus was the first of Ernest Bradbury's courses on the Appreciation of Films, which predated the long standing programme of film studies at Swarthmore but sadly was a one-off at this time. Another new direction after the war was the beginning of the local history and landscape studies represented by courses on the Yorkshire Dales and especially Maurice Beresford's course on Scenery as History.

## Settlement to Centre

Important constitutional and administrative changes were also in train. Swarthmore dropped its founding title of 'Settlement' and became a 'Centre' for the first time, which probably reflected the greater say civic powers had in its financing. This was represented in the balance sheet of £1769 for 1945 which showed £513 from the Ministry of Education and £358 from Leeds LEA, which combined at nearly 50% of income and now just outweighed the £295 grants from Friends' trusts' total and student fees of £486, an important shift of funding. It also adopted a constitution which now formally made it a student democracy by permitting the direct election of students onto the Executive Committee. Swarthmore was also represented on the Leeds University and WEA Joint Committee for the first time, which severely ruffled the feathers of some old-timers in the WEA and was to lead to a break with the WEA in 1951 that lasted until 1959, as we shall see.

With Neill's departure in 1946, the new Warden was Maurice Hughes. Shortly after he arrived, however, Swarthmore's landlord marked the occasion in cataclysmic style by giving notice to quit to 4 Woodhouse Square. But the friends of Swarthmore rallied – as Steinitz later remarked, Swarthmore always transformed a crisis into an opportunity – and after intensive lobbying, the landlord relented and offered to extend the lease by five more years. The new climate of reconstruction and determination not to allow the old social order to restore its worst abuses brought about an enthusiasm for 'world citizenship', an idea that had been kindled by Swarthmore's internationalism of the inter-war period when a hunger for understanding other peoples had been a rich motivation. Post-war planning was also prominent and courses like International Economic Relations flourished. This was the title of the first Extension lecture course to be offered by the newly formed Dept. of Extra Mural Studies at Leeds University. A visit from the new Vice-Chancellor, Charles Morris, cemented a long standing relationship with the University's extra-mural provision.

The creation of the Extra-Mural Department under Sidney Raybould created a decisively new context for relations with the University. Previously, as we have seen, these had been managed through its provision of tutorial classes through its Joint Committee which George Thompson the WEA's redoubtable District Secretary, regarded as his personal fiefdom. The Extension lecture programme was the way by which Sidney Raybould, the first Director of the new Extra Mural Dept., took back some control over University provision from the WEA. As a consequence more arts based courses were provided by the University, though its provision of social sciences, politics and social history began inexorably to dwindle. Thompson, who had been District Secretary with a break of six years in the 1920s since the district's foundation in 1914, resigned in 1946. He was replaced by Fred Sedgwick who in his own milder way was to become equally influential in WEA affairs both in Yorkshire and at the national level.

Another of Swarthmore's pioneers, Edmund Harvey, resigned as Chair of the Council in 1944 and was succeeded by his brother Prof. John W Harvey, keeping the family interest intact. However with the resignation of Edwin Rowntree, the Treasurer, and Gervase Ford the link with the founding Quaker generation was weakened substantially. In 1949 Hughes resigned after $3\frac{1}{2}$ years to take up a post at Darlington Training College and Geoffrey Hines became Warden.

**Maurice Hughes**

Warden 1946-1949. Previously a resident at the Mary Ward Settlement in London and subsequently a WEA Tutor Organiser in Dorset and then the Army Education Corps. Hughes was an economist with a particular interest in community development, serving on the Leeds and District Federation of Community Associations.

## Geoffrey Hines

Warden: 1949-1959. Scholarly follower of T.S. Eliot with whom he began a correspondence and from whom he received four letters 1956-60 now in Hayward Bequest, Cambridge. Eliot was then courting his second wife, Valerie Fletcher, who lived in Weetwood Lane, Headingley. Hines opened up a rift with WEA, which he tried to fill by encouraging a higher academic quality from Swarthmore's independent programme and the University called Progressive Tutorial Classes. He developed a major expansion of the winter programme to around 70 courses and a regular summer programme completed his desire for a 36 week academic year, in line with the Ashby Report proposals. Membership rose to around 1500. Resigned in August 1959 to become Warden of the Bristol Folk House

## Hines and the Rift with the WEA

Hines introduced a remarkably new tone to the Centre and considerable innovation. Almost immediately however, relations with the WEA over the provision of the Joint Committee classes broke down and, for whatever reason, were not to be repaired swiftly. Swarthmore's 1950-51 Annual Report (ironically, illustrated by John Mansbridge, who was the son of the WEA's founder Albert Mansbridge) regretting the break, seemed to suggest the WEA was its author. Hines noted: 'The continuance of Tutorial classes run through the Leeds Branch of the WEA, gave rise to difficulties which resulted in the termination of a long partnership. We accept with sorrow a decision we did not seek and take this opportunity to extend our good wishes to the Branch'. Was this another crisis or an opportunity to be seized? Hines's reaction seems to suggest the latter and he immediately took steps to imprint his own mark on the Centre. He formed what was called a Panel on Academic Policy to fill the vacuum and 'to achieve balance' of the whole programme. Significantly for the first time, this included regular meetings of class secretaries and the Student Committee.

Hines's approach contrasted markedly with that of Hughes, the social scientist. He came from a literary and philosophical background and was fond of citing the work of the celebrated poet, T S Eliot, his first report eruditely (but obscurely) quoting from his Four Quartets on the need for the constant 'raid on the inarticulate'. Could this be this Leeds? Hines described it as 'a city whose smoky pall but camouflages an independent and active culture' (curiously echoing the sentiments of Alfred Orage and Holbrook Jackson when they founded the Leeds Arts Club nearly fifty years earlier). He also quoted from Winston Churchill on the need for 'free men studying with free minds', which suggests something of the Cold War ethos creeping in. Later he much admired the contribution of the conservative social philosopher Michael Oakeshott and quoted approvingly from his inaugural lecture at LSE. Oakeshott held that education was 'neither fixed nor finished...it has no changeless centre to which understanding can anchor itself; there is no sovereign purpose to be perceived nor invariable direction to be detected'. Hines also seemed to take to heart Oakeshott's injunction that education should contain 'a principle of continuity' in which 'authority is diffused between past, present, and future...a concrete coherent manner of living in all its intricateness'. Again this may suggest a passion for the arcane on Hines's part but may well be a swipe at what he may have perceived as WEA dogmatism and a need for a less ideological approach.

Practically, Hines was also well aware of the new currents in adult education emanating from national reports and other centres of influence, which meant that Swarthmore could no longer take its independence from national policy for granted. In the 1953-54 annual report he quotes from the government's Report on Adult Education (1954), chaired by Eric Ashby, on the importance of voluntarism in adult education and its emphasis on the need for a high quality of students, teaching and subject content. Ashby's report, the first national inquiry on adult education since the war, had more or less agreed that adult education should be left alone by government except for greater involvement of the local LEA. However, the report was concerned that not all classes were of a high enough standard to merit state funding, and it was clear that without firm university support, Swarthmore with its increasing reliance on languages and arts and crafts, might not make the grade.

Indeed there was a problem, since the academic ballast had in the immediate past been provided by the WEA, either directly in one year classes or through its historic control of the university's Joint Committee programme. But with George Thompson's retirement and the creation of the new Extra Mural Department under Sidney Raybould, there was an opportunity to start afresh. The break with the WEA may have been a manifestation of this, maybe not sought but not mourned either. Hines also agreed with Harold Wiltshire from Nottingham's Extra Mural Department on the need to sustain 'a small minority of reflective citizens', which pre-empted what Richard Hoggart was to say in his *Uses of Literacy* (1957) about the 'earnest minority'. For good measure Hines also agreed with Vice-Chancellor Charles Morris on education's need for serious reflection – 'the thinker who has no traffic with the depths can do little more than teach a trick or two'. Swarthmore might have been seen as overly dependent on handicrafts and the performing arts but 'lantern slide' tours of the humanities would not fit the bill either.

### Progressive Tutorial Classes

Hines's solution was to create, in 1954, what he called Progressive Tutorial Classes 'after some years of experiment' with the co-operation of the LEA and the ESA. In effect he tried to replicate the serious arts and social science classes previously organised and funded through the WEA, with funding from other sources. But they were also innovative in the sense that they eschewed an abstract or overly theoretical approach for a more pragmatic problem-based approach (on the lines then being advocated by the Scottish philosopher John Macmurray, of thought as essentially a reflection on action).

Transmitting radio demonstration, c. 1950

This was genuinely exciting and, ironically, a revitalising of the spirit of the original WEA tutorial tradition. Despite the fact that his own approach might be considered not totally impartial, Hines clearly encouraged a break from ideological approaches to education. He reported with satisfaction that in 1955 the Swarthmore annual tutors conference wanted to replace the 'isms' of the pre-war period with a more practical approach as suggested by modern philosophy's approach to language to which Stephen Toulmin, then Professor of Philosophy at Leeds, gave support in his address.

In practice, however, this meant students had to work harder! The need for a problem-based rather than 'lantern slide' approach to classes in such classes as archaeology, astronomy and ornithology denied students the opportunity simply to relax and passively enjoy them. Many were deterred and numbers fell. Nevertheless, to Hines's evident relief, a 'good core' of 800 remained prepared to do the more exacting work of interpretation in the arts and humanities. However, following discussions by Swarthmore's education panel and tutors' conference on new ways of presenting subjects, he was stretching a point when he remarked in the next annual report that had the philosopher Ludwig Wittgenstein looked in on one of our meetings, he might have said 'What you have primarily discovered is a new way of looking at things'. Some might have regarded this a little high falutin'.

Other matters weighed heavily too. The death of Frank Archer of the Students' Committee while walking near Malham removed a valuable prop to the Centre's work. Then there was the major problem caused in 1956 by the Ministry of Education's decision, without prior consultation with the voluntary bodies, to impose a dramatic increase in fees. Leeds compensated by raising its grant to £900 but membership fell sharply (not helped by the new tougher study regime) and did not recover for the next two years. Swarthmore's annual expenditure had now risen to £3317 of which a little under half was covered by fees. The trusts including James Reckitt's, Brotherton's and Henry Clay's and the University of Leeds's contribution made up the rest. But it was clear now that greater state support increasingly compromised Swarthmore's autonomy. A further issue was one of space. Even with maximum use of the building the seams creaked and without immediate expansion, classes would have to be held in the street.

As it was, outlying buildings were used for dance and other classes but an attempt at reviving outreach classes in Hunslet failed. The 'Friends of Swarthmore' was inaugurated in 1954, to raise income and goodwill and with the generosity of Councillor Bernard Lyons an extension was opened. Lyons whose father had founded the Alexandre tailoring firm, which he now ran, had once lived in 3 Woodhouse Square, of which he had fond memories. Because of Swarthmore's dedication to internationalism and an open door to Jewish refugees, Lyons became its greatest benefactor and few years later made possible the purchase of his old home. This marks the era of the permanent appeal for funds which was to become a leitmotif and a new hall was proposed at a cost of £3800. The response to the appeal was good with Lyons, Leeds City Council and the Friends each giving £1000; while Leeds LICS, Tetley and the University gave £100 each. Originally 'a place for Friends', Swarthmore could always rely on its friends drawn from much broader circles.

Did Hines's reforms work? The programme of classes during the 1950s was certainly interesting and innovative but it relied essentially on the continuation of a core of language classes, handicrafts and dance with a scattering of humanities courses. The biggest single post-war casualty was the programme of social sciences. While Neill and Hughes had in their time valiantly promoted courses in economics, politics, sociology, social history and related subjects, the rift with the WEA and Hines's own predilections for philosophy and literature reduced them to vestigial traces. Another reason for the decline in social sciences may have been the proportion of women now attending classes. Historically, women had always been in the minority in social science classes and were to be found in greater numbers in the humanities and arts and crafts. At the end of the war women now exceeded men by 3 to 1 although this declined to 2 to 1 by 1962 (Hanna, 1964). The only 'social' science to take root under Hines was psychology, which sometimes occupied three evenings of the programme. As we have seen this trend was inspired by Harry Guntrip during the war but he no longer took classes. But another warmly remembered tutor took up the baton. This was Reg Marks whose classes focused on how the individual adapted to everyday life and fitted in to social life, which provided the entry point for many new stalwarts, like Marjorie Hall, to Swarthmore's collective life.

Although there were regular political forums and debates in which prominent academics and members of political parties, including the Communist Party, would put forward their points of view for discussion, Hines personally appeared to eschew politics; it may have been significant that his own contribution to one such forum was confined to a concluding session which was entitled 'Confound their politics!' in 1951. There were also courses on Local Government, a Housing Policy forum, a Child Study group and Current Affairs. Philosophy also maintained its prominent place, sometimes with three classes in one week by Professors Harvey and Davison, and Hines's own class on Plato's Republic. Stephen Toulmin later taught a course on modern philosophical problems and Roy Shaw, who was a member of the Extra-Mural Department, taught a class on Social Philosophy on the University's Extension programme. Another high flyer, Shaw later became Head of the Adult Education Department at the newly formed Keele University and was subsequently chairman of the Arts Council.

A more serious approach too was taken to English social history, though this appeared in the coronation year of 1953 as a distinctly reverential History of the Crown. TS Eliot once remarked that he was a Classicist in poetry an Anglican in religion and a Royalist in politics and Hines may well have taken the same view. The 1951 Festival of Britain programme was conclusively a celebration of 'heritage' and empire which was reflected, without the least irony, in a residential course at Grantley Hall in 1954 on 'Western responsibilities to backward peoples'. But a rising feature of the programme was local studies and for the first time there were courses on the History of the Yorkshire Dales, which included a contribution from the celebrated Dales historian, Arthur Raistrick, and the Story of Leeds taught by Maurice Beresford. These were courses in which students did active research in local archives and became a great success. The first of Mrs. Foster of the Thoresby Society's essential classes on Palaeography was given in 1956. Another return to the programme was religious studies with the Rev. Lee offering a series of classes on Jesus, the Old Testament and the Prophets. The link with the Adult School activists, who in the early days would have relished the class, was thin, their numbers having sunk from 600 during the war to 111 in 1962–63 in line with national trends (Hanna, 1964). Lee also offered one of the few social science classes on the Economics of Everyday Life.

The other key humanities subject to maintain its place on the syllabus was English literature although perhaps surprisingly it was the Marxist literary critic and life-long Communist, Arnold Kettle (father of the *Guardian*'s Martin Kettle), who was the most regular university tutor. His most famous work *An Introduction to the English Novel* (1951–53) was a product of his devotion to adult education and he became the first Professor of English Literature in the Open University in 1970. Douglas Jefferson, a much loved lecturer in the School of English at Leeds and prominent Henry James specialist also contributed. Hines himself taught a course on his beloved Eliot with whom by 1957 he was communicating regularly – they may even have been introduced to each other by Bonamy Dobree, a friend of Eliot's.

### Languages, Arts and Crafts – and Rambling and Mating

The core of Swarthmore's programme was nevertheless still languages, the arts and crafts, and dancing which occupied a good half the programme. Tina Tomasini added Italian and became a resident, while Mrs. Mendel took over the French classes started by Jean Inebnit. Martha Steinitz continued to teach four or five course a week although now her sister shared the burden. Steinitz was also lecturing regularly on Art Appreciation, including classes on Van Gogh, and appeared in a number of other guises, though no longer with courses on the Jews and anti-Semitism. She regularly translated German plays into English including Goethe's *Faust*, which was performed by the Swarthmore Players in 1951, and wrote plays for performance by her advanced German class. Her adaptation of Thomas Mann's great novel *Buddenbrooks* into a play even won the approval of Mann himself, it was said. Her plays were also being published and she had begun to attract a considerable reputation for her contribution to the Arts, eventually receiving and honorary MA from Leeds University in 1961.

She had taught in Swarthmore now for over 30 years and had attracted a dedicated following. Moreover she had taken one of the fundamental threads of the Settlement, internationalism, and made it a living reality. She was practically a one-woman League of Nations, noting the 'waves of invasions by Jewish refugees' in the 1930s which she said 'threatened to swallow up the normal life of Swarthmore' (Steinitz, (1959) *Swarthmore 1959 Jubilee History*: 25).

Buddenbrooks:. Performance of Martha Steinitz's adaptation of the Thomas Mann novel.
Above Toni and Permaneder greet one another. "Ja, die Frau Grünlich!"
Below author and producer Martha Steinitz and Warden Geoffrey Hines take a bow.

But despite Allott's concerns, Swarthmore students went out of their way to befriend the students and nourished the centre as a home for the temporarily homeless. After the war she noted how displaced persons flocked to Swarthmore to learn English and about English culture and it became a kind of People's High School. It was she said 'a little world full of devotion, human kindness and optimism' (Ibid).

The expansion of the arts and crafts programme was very much driven by student demand and now included for the first time classes on Clay Modelling and Pottery by Audrey Pearson, Swarthmore now possessing the first of its kilns. Joseph Appleyard developed the painting and sketching courses into a major feature of the programme, which frequently took students out into the country for *plein aire* work. Embroidery, taught by Mrs E. M. Stewart and Miss K. Birch, now replaced basket-making and weaving as the most popular handicraft. Calligraphy was also taught for few years.

But for the more energetic, Folk Dancing – English, Scottish, Morris and Sword – also occupied several evenings and for a few years ballet was added, although taught in a school near Kirkgate Market.

Although the Arts were Hines's first love, the science programme also ticked over and newcomers to the syllabus included a class on Electric Tubes and one on the Maths of Radio, provided by the Leeds Radio Club, which continued to use Swarthmore as its base and offered a constant source of innovative thinking on new technology. Mary Hesse also gave a class on Science and Your Faith, possibly for the doubters, while the first of Arthur Gilpin's remarkable Ornithology classes began in 1953 and were to remain on the programme for the next 30 years.

But what made Swarthmore more than just an educational centre was its social life. As we have seen it nurtured a number of clubs for rambling, cycling, nature study, photography and radio enthusiasts. Its Saturday socials attracted a regular following and, by maintaining a Common Room with a coffee bar, it gave the opportunity for chance meetings and interdisciplinary discussion. The Student Committee also organised frequent weekends away, whose less academic pursuits were immensely popular with Swarthmore's younger folk, as may be imagined. But nature disposed that they formed two self selecting groups, the singles opting for the Coop Holiday Association (CHA) hostel, nicknamed the 'Catch Husbands Association', while married couples favoured the Holidays Fellowship Association (HFA) or 'Husbands Found Association' (Hines, 1997 letter quoted in Bennett and Hall, 1999).

After rambling and mating however, play-reading and performance were the singly most popular recreational pursuits and Swarthmore Playgoers had a deserved reputation for fine performances. Under Elspeth Whitaker, who lived in the top floor flat further down Woodhouse Square, novices were encouraged to read from sight and lay their nerves aside. One student echoed the sentiments of many when she described her as a 'gifted and exceptional lady' who 'could charm a note from the throat of a bird and – if you were in one of her productions – a flicker of an eyelash from you'. Performances were held regularly in Swarthmore itself for socials and before larger gatherings at the Friends Meeting House on Carlton Hill and once at Armley Gaol. Students made props and costumes, did the lighting, learned stagecraft and occasionally found themselves auditioning for the BBC, rehearsing long into the night. When Elspeth Whitaker left to become full-time Drama Adviser to schools around the country, an era of thespian success drew to a close.

## The Post War Settlement

By the time Hines resigned in August 1959 to become Warden of the Bristol Folk House, the winter programme had grown to around 70 courses, a phenomenal expansion, and there was a regular summer programme which completed his desire for a 36 week academic year, in line with the Ashby Report proposals. Membership rose to around 1500 despite the government imposed increase in fees of almost 50% and Swarthmore had become a genuine student democracy with an ever active Students' Committee and a newly formed Theatrical Group. Hines was also vindicated by a very good HMI report, the first of many, in which the inspectors visited 37 and 38 classes in each of two weeks and were very pleased not only with atmosphere among students but by the academic quality of the work.

Now no longer a Settlement but a 'Centre', Swarthmore had undoubtedly lost a great deal of its founding connection with the Quaker Friends, although some still remained on the Council, and had transformed itself into an independent educational centre supported by the local authority. This was in large part due to Butler's 1944 Education Act which had laid responsibilities on LEAs for adult education which Leeds, prompted by Hines's predecessor, Desmond Neill, had

Swarthmore signs up its 1000th Student, James McKelvie, in 1957. James, left, is watched by Warden Geoffrey Hines and Miss Gertrude Meadows.

honoured royally. Overall Leeds LEA increased its grant by 15% in 1945, happily combining, as Councillor Happold remarked, 'public money with voluntary effort' (Happold 1959, *Jubilee Report:* 23). But the withdrawal of the ECA's annual grant of £350 (on the grounds that Swarthmore could now stand on its own feet and the money could more beneficially used in funding new ventures) prompted another deputation from Swarthmore to the Council in 1946. Leeds agreed to pay tutors' salaries on recognised classes and to grant aid administrative costs to the tune of £100, subject to audited accounts. This rapidly quintupled to £500 by 1950 and by the end of the following decade trebled again to around £1500. Salaries of staff rose to £3,600. On top of this Leeds gave grants for renovation of buildings and equipment and £1,000 for the new hall in 1958. Thus Swarthmore was now a key part of the LEA adult education provision, for many the jewel in the crown. But, in a burst of Delphic utterance not usually associated with elected members, Councillor Happold noted it had become a rather different institution: 'Perhaps it no longer meets the needs of the educationally starved but…those whose appetite has already been whetted' (Happold, (1959) *Jubilee Report*: 24). The feeling amongst some councillors that Swarthmore now served a more middle-class clientele returned to blight relations two decades later, as we shall see in the next chapter.

Its closer dependence on the City Council meant Swarthmore had lost considerable control over its fees but however retained considerable autonomy over provision, now increasingly student driven. Hines struggled to maintain its academic quality which had been weakened by the break with the WEA and, although many took their bat home, his policy seemed to have worked. The rift was healed by the time he left (or possibly even because he left) but it was for his successor to reap the benefits. Hines's other great achievement had been to formalise non-statutory financial support into the Friends of Swarthmore organisation, although independent benefactors like Bernard Lyons still played an immense role. Swarthmore had become a key feature in the adult educational culture of Leeds and attracted widespread goodwill. Even in the frost of the Cold War, the invasion of Hungary and the revelation of Stalin's crimes in Khrushchev's speech, Hines still permitted a significant left wing and even Communist presence in Swarthmore despite his own more conservative instincts, a celebration of its openness.

Swarthmore's Jubilee in 1959 provoked a period of reflection. Hewitson noted how the war had accelerated the change from the founders' commitment to the religious training of the working man to a more comprehensive programme of a wider a public (Hewitson 1959: 20). Working men by 1960 were less than a third of its membership, which was increasingly drawn from the lower end of the professional spectrum, with many teachers, white collar workers and housewives attending classes. There were now twice as many women as men and over 1500 students regularly attended classes (compared with the constant 200 or so until about 1920). But according to Ian Hanna, who investigated the adult education scene in Leeds in 1961–62 and visited Swarthmore frequently, demographic changes could not in themselves account for the large post-war increase in enrolments. One relatively new group was middle-aged housewives, who had missed out on higher education earlier, but in language and Joint Committee tutorial classes the average age was 10 years younger. Overall, Swarthmore had kept a youthful clientele from earliest times, indicating in part that the self-improvement ethic was still strong, many students rising above their class origins (Hanna, 1964). Hence although the clientele was largely 'lower professional' probably the majority were only one generation away from working-class origins. But it was Hanna's view that the individualistic approach that stressed competition between students and discriminatory qualifications, could not possible fit Swarthmore's enduring ethos of fellowship: '[the] personal self advancement attitude did not achieve anything for most people in school, and is not a motivation in their daily work, their family environment or their leisure. *For these people the better assumed values would be collectivist rather than individual work or writing*' (Ibid p 230, my emphasis). Many Swarthmore regulars would say amen to that, but the sixties had arrived and everything would change. The era of austerity fellowship that was passing was signalled by a wonderful pastiche of Kipling's poem 'If' in the Wartime Log Book by Frank Glover, almost a kind of epitaph:

Swarthmore Coffee Bar, 1950s

If you can use your leisure in the evenings,
To come to Swarthmore wet or fine,
If you can study French or Economics,
And argue after class till half past nine;
If you can do your homework without grousing,
And read the books your tutor recommends,
If you can disagree with other students,
And yet remain the best of friends.

If you can show your merit in the kitchen,
In washing up and making cups of tea,
If you can hold your own in conversation,
And say so, when you feel you disagree;
If you can spend some Sundays with the ramblers,
And always promptly catch the eight-three train,
If you can walk all day with brand new shoes on,
And never say a word about the pain.

If you can do your duty in committee,
To speak up for the things you think are right,
If you can show your willingness to reason,
Yet not accept defeat without a fight;
If you can join in all the fun at Socials,
And do your best to make the party go,
If you can give the tea and cakes out,
And stand aside when food is running low,

If you can act as 'Host' in open evenings,
And use your charm to keep the party bright,
If you can spend an hour in the library,
To dust the books and put them back just right,
If you believe sincerely, that what matters,
Is not what you receive – but what you give,
The Swarthmore's yours, and everything that's in it,
And which is more – You're learning how to live!

## CHAPTER 5

# The Making of a Radical Arts Centre, 1960–1973

**Brian Stapleton**

Brian Stapleton was the son of teachers in North Yorkshire, he was schooled in Bootham and Ayton but, on his own account, having had quite enough of education by 1939, he ran away to join the Civil Service. He was a conscientious objector in the second world war, where he claimed to have discovered "real work" as a hospital orderly (Mike Stapleton, 2006) and spent some time working for the Sheffield Council for Refugees, becoming Warden of the International Centre there. After two further years acting in a travelling theatre group, he was awarded a grant to attend the London School of Economics (LSE), where he met his wife to be. In a remarkable break from traditional male roles, he looked after his son Michael as a baby, earning a living from drama work in London youth clubs while his wife studied for her own degree. Following graduation, he became Tutor Organiser for the WEA in Lincolnshire but then in 1953 with a family of two boys, he joined the new University College of Ibadan, in Northern Nigeria as an extra-mural tutor.

In 1959 Swarthmore's first half century was marked in some style with Jubilee celebrations held at Leeds University and the Civic Hall, an art exhibition opened by the Director of Leeds Art Gallery, Robert Rowe. Ron Forbes Adams of the National Institute of Adult Education (NIAE) gave a talk on the Future of Adult Education. The Students' Committee published a *Jubilee Magazine* edited by Len Ludlam, which attempted to encapsulate the Centre's essential history in a series of articles by those who had played formative roles, such as Gerald Hibbert and Martha Steinitz and included a very valuable assessment by B. Hewitson of its contribution to the City of Leeds. Swarthmore had much to celebrate but also a little to mourn. Hines's departure was followed by the deaths of the long-term caretaker William Poel and the art teacher, Joseph Appleyard, who had done much to establish Swarthmore's reputation for practical art classes. In 1963 a new post of Assistant Warden was created and filled by the enthusiastic Tom Costello. Membership, then at about 1600, was shortly to pass the 2000 mark, while Swarthmore's expenditure was to double by the end of the decade, much to the consternation of the LEA. The times were a-changing, rent by the swelling upsurge in 'Americanised' popular culture, assaults on traditional standards and eventually student rebellion, on a roller coaster of youthful exuberance and for many older members, some exasperation.

Geoffrey Hines was succeeded in 1959 by a very different character in the shape of Brian Stapleton, who was to serve as Warden for the next five years. Although Hines did not at all lack a social consciousness, Stapleton returned to Swarthmore some of the radical pioneering spirit of its founders. The rift with the WEA was healed and relations with Leeds LEA seemed to have entered a period of all-round good will and financial stability. Swarthmore was 'full to overflowing', according to its 1959–60 Annual Report, and the future looked bright. Hines had indeed laid a firm basis for progress relying on a very substantial languages programme – now providing a third of all post-school provision in the City of Leeds – and a blossoming liberal arts programme. What it lacked as we have seen, was an equally strong social science component, which Stapleton, with the backing of Fred Sedgwick, the WEA's District Secretary, now also renting offices in Swarthmore, began to remedy. In the 1960–61 Annual Report, he openly regretted the decline in social sciences classes which he said, bluntly, were due to not facing up to the 'vital human issues of the day'.

## The Return of the WEA and the Social Sciences

Stapleton, himself, taught courses on Africa and its problems and supplemented them at one stage with a course called My Africa, taught by black Africans (possibly a first for Swarthmore) on their own experiences and understanding, which extended Swarthmore's reputation for cosmopolitanism even further. Given that the Cold War with the Soviet bloc was still a sensitive issue, a politically combative view was given by Fred Singleton's course on the 'Peoples' Democracies' – the Communist states of Eastern Europe – which attempted to read them in a more sympathetic light. A further boost to the social sciences programme was given by Eric Butterworth, who initiated a Joint Committee class on the Study of Society. The Leeds-born Butterworth (1929-2006) was fast emerging as one of Britain's leading sociologists and his text books became some of the most frequently referenced works for a generation of sociology students. There were also new courses on the Law and the Citizen and Political Philosophy. Another incipient *globalista* was Alastair Macintyre, who led an Advanced Tutorial course in philosophy (this was the fourth year added on to a three year university tutorial class). Macintyre's book *After Virtue* (1981) made him one of the most internationally-respected ethical philosophers of his generation. Another well-established philosopher, A. J. Kenny, a medieval specialist, also taught in the Centre.

The study of religion also began something of a renaissance, although with a sceptical bent, the Rev. Elms, for example, holding classes on Existentialism and Religious Belief in which traditional authority was subjected to hard questioning. A quite new direction was signalled in courses on practical economics such as the economics of the wool trade and even,

**Brian Stapleton** continued

Nigeria was then on the brink of its longed-for Independence from Britain (1 October 1960) led by vibrant nationalist movements and Stapleton followed up what had been a pioneering adult educational movement spearheaded by another Quaker, Tommy Hodgkin of the Oxford University Delegacy (Oxford's Extra Mural Department). Hodgkin's work, which had in truth been simply concerned with educating an indigenous democratic leadership for Nigeria, was roundly denounced as a Communist conspiracy in the House of Lords (Fieldhouse, 1986: 61). During this period Stapleton wrote a well-received book entitled 'The Wealth of Nigeria' (1958). After six years Stapleton and family returned to Yorkshire to take up the Swarthmore job but did not leave his concern for Africa behind. The family home in Horsforth, according to his son, was shared with an assortment of overseas student lodgers and it soon became a hub the Anti-Apartheid Movement in the North of England.

puzzlingly, of pig farming. Stapleton himself taught classes on everyday economics, even venturing into popular culture by taking as an example for study that long-haired 'beat combo', The Beatles, who, as one of their songs at the time made clear, were very keen *not* to share their increasingly fabulous incomes with the taxman. Reg Marks, whose warmth and personality attracted a wide following, continued to teach Psychology.

It was also clear that Stapleton had a well-defined view of how Swarthmore as an independent adult education centre should work to its strengths. In an article for the journal *Adult Education* in 1964, he outlined the virtues of the co-operative planning of adult education and in integrating the official, voluntary and informal education, which made Swarthmore, a 'laboratory of adult education practices' (Stapleton, 1964). It was something of a timely intervention in the debate about adult education policy then raging in which those who wished to modernise the field insisted that centres should become more specialist and concentrate on a *narrower* curriculum. This was a sign of the times, sadly, that heralded the unreflective functionalism much beloved of later policy makers. Stapleton argued, on the contrary, in favour of a 'Grand Comprehensive Adult education Centre' in which you could:

> *in the same environment do art and art appreciation in the same or successive years, find yourself involved in discussion with photographers and language students studying the culture of different nations, and plan joint expeditions with archaeologists and botanists. The meeting points of different disciplines become a reality and the stimulus provided act outwards to other more exclusive environments.* (Stapleton, 1964: 15)

Such a centre could flourish, Stapleton continued, only with an active partnership between all the providing agencies including the LEA, the WEA and the University. He was absolutely insistent that specialisation and segregation were simply not in tune with adult needs, whatever the economically-minded modernisers wanted. However, although undoubtedly following the path of virtue, such a stance was to put Swarthmore increasingly out on a limb as far as the new managerial ethos was concerned.

THE MAKING OF A RADICAL ARTS CENTRE, 1960–1973

Geoffrey Hines, right, hands over to new Swarthmore Warden Brian Stapleton, left, 1959

Stapleton effectively built on Hines's decade of consolidation, with languages at the core and a growing engagement with the practical Arts alongside a renewed commitment to social sciences. This very much laid the basis for Swarthmore's curricular balance for the following decades and the reinstatement of the WEA/Leeds University Joint Committee programme gave it substantial academic credibility. While old favourites like Edward Pybus's Music classes re-appeared on the programme, new university tutors included Charlie Johnson who taught literature, Percy Boynton teaching History and, on the University Extension programme, the celebrated Catholic literary critic, Walter Stein, on Religious Drama, while George Hauger taught on the York Mystery Plays and Roy Shaw on Culture and Society. All were to continue 'in residence' for many years.

Drama and the practical arts flourished, the Swarthmore Players giving regular performances, often with experimental material like Pirandello's *Six Characters in Search of an Author* as well as Ivor Novello's *Nude with a Violin* (no doubt to greater crowds), making full use of the permanent stage in the new hall extension, which was completed in 1963. York Unity Theatre also performed Arnold Wesker's daringly 'kitchen sink' drama *Chicken Soup with Barley* in 1964 and for the first time a professional theatre group took up the new stage. This was 'Theatre Roundabout' who performed *For Crying Out Loud*, described as a 'kaleidoscope of Christian virtues'. But a growing trend was in showing the art work of both tutors and students and also travelling Arts Council exhibitions in Swarthmore. Joe Appleyard's place was taken by a panel of talented new tutors that included John Jones, Diane Thubron and Molly Lord, who became one of Swarthmore's most enduring tutors, warmly admired for her commitment to students' expressive work. In 1962–63 no less than twelve exhibitions were displayed including Arthur Gilpin's nature photography and one from the Contemporary Arts Society.

Dancing, basketry, embroidery, and handwriting were still popular as were photography, pottery, playing the recorder, and speech training. Amongst the new subjects on offer were the first of Les Reyner's Film Appreciation courses that remained on the programme for nearly thirty years. Art History also had an interesting revival in the shape of course such as From Futurism to N. F. Simpson taught by Frederick May and Picasso and Others by John Jones.

Swarthmore kept up the tradition of science courses that had been present from earliest years, with courses on bird watching, plants, animals, and geomorphology, the latter backed up by a residential course at Grantley Hall on Life in the Landscape. But in another programme innovation, courses on architecture and city life took shape, with a path-breaking study of suburban life by the architectural historian, Alison Ravetz. She was to become a crusading figure in Leeds civic life over the following decades and highly influential to the process of changing the local authority approach to conservation – her iconoclastic books *Model Estate* (1974) and *Remaking Cities* (1980) became essential reading for all students of architecture and town planning. Her American husband, the celebrated Philosopher of Science, Jerry Ravetz, who had attended Swarthmore College in Philadelphia as a young man, also taught courses.

Practically-orientated classes began to appear like Public Speaking for Trade Unionists and Early Retirement, taught by Stan Cook. This may well have owed something to the Edmund Harvey Memorial lecture given by Ellen McCullough, then President of the WEA and Women's Officer for the Transport and General Workers' Union. There were also afternoon classes in Home Design and Gardening. The languages programme continued to be centred in French, Italian and German, the latter still commanded by the Steinitz sisters, Martha and Hedwig. There was also a renewal of the courses on Jewish History (but not this time given by Martha Steinitz). Esperanto still had a foothold and English for Foreigners was very popular but the new kids on the block were Modern Greek and Russian (for the optimists, it was said). On the Joint Committee programme the first course in Archaeology was offered by Vincent Bellamy, while Tom Caldwell concentrated on the History of Leeds. The celebrated local historian, Bernard Jennings, well-know for his WEA class's seminal History of Nidderdale (1967) began a tutorial class on the History of Yorkshire. Jennings later became Professor of Adult Education in Hull and a popular President of the WEA.

Perhaps the most interesting sign of the times was the rise of the courses in Writing for Pleasure, introduced for the first time by Bill Price Turner. These were 'full to overflowing' and rapidly established Turner as a new icon in Swarthmore's pantheon.

**Bill Price Turner**

Bill Price Turner was born in York, and succeeded Jon Silkin as the Gregory Fellow in Poetry at the University of Leeds, 1960-1962, where he was very popular and noted for the 'encouragement and assistance ... given to nearly every student writer in the University'. Between 1962 and 1966 he worked as a sub-editor, and then as a crime fiction reviewer for the 'Yorkshire Post', while teaching creative writing classes at Swarthmore. One of his most celebrated collections of poetry, 'The Moral Rocking Horse', was the product of these years. Very much a practical poet with little time for literary criticism, Turner's view, as expressed in the programme, was that 'a little experience of life was more useful that a tower of theory'.

## The Problems of Growth

Once again Swarthmore had to expand its premises to cope with the growth in classes and, after a successful appeal, bought number 5 Woodhouse Square, while Leeds City Council purchased numbers 6 and 7 and leased them on a pepper-corn rent. By 1962 number 5 was integrated, with a flat for the new caretaker in the attic. However rather unexpectedly, Stapleton resigned from the Wardenship in 1964 to take up a post in Denmark as Head of a Rural Development College. Maybe the fact that Swarthmore's annual expenditure had suddenly leapt by over £2,000 to a yearly figure of around £9,600, leaving the Centre deeply in debt to the LEA, played a part in his decision. At the beginning of his period as Warden, funding for classes had altered decisively in favour of the local authority and in a sense it had reached a climacteric. The annual grant for administration had now risen to around £1400 (from the original £100 agreed in 1946 when Leeds took on the burden for adult education outlined in the Butler 1944 Education Act) and paid £3600 for staff salaries making a total of £5,000. On top of that Leeds had contributed £848 for alterations to the premises and another £1000 for the hall extension. At the end of Stapleton's six years the Centre's membership nudged the 2,000 mark and had recovered many of its social passions but there was no doubt the piper had to be paid.

His successor, Brian Thompson, entered this new relationship with the City fathers as Warden in 1964 with a characteristic flourish, maintaining that the business of the Warden at Swarthmore was to hold the balance between three providers of classes: the LEA, the University and the WEA. His assertion that no less than 25% of the students were in the more academically rigorous classes of the WEA and the University and the Centre was not merely 'a hobbyists' hideaway' (Annual Report 1964-5) prompts speculation that some in the Council might have thought otherwise. Thompson recognised Swarthmore's closer relationship with the City but was determined nevertheless to maintain its unique character: 'Adult education is primarily and essentially a local and immediate phenomenon. A good-sized room, warm, well-lit, with a sensitive tutor interested in helping students realize their personal best – this is still the best and only pattern of our kind of education', he claimed (Annual Report, 1965-66). But the centre of gravity in Swarthmore, as he recognised, was its languages courses, which led to cultural understanding and on the strength of this he proposed to create a Centre for European Studies.

It was also something of a coup to attract the leading social historian, Asa Briggs, to give the Edmund Harvey Memorial Lecture in 1964. Born in Keighley, from 1955 until 1961 he had been Professor of Modern History at the University of Leeds. He then moved on to the University of Sussex, where he became Vice-Chancellor (1967–76). Briggs was also passionate about adult education and in 1978 became Chancellor of the Open University. He gave a stimulating talk on the New Universities in which he confirmed the enduring need for the liberal, cross disciplinary studies in the arts and sciences that had traditionally marked Swarthmore's curriculum.

But the growth of the Centre now questioned whether it was still in line with this ideal. Growth required a larger administrative staff. With the resignation of Tom Costello as Assistant Warden, his place was taken by Richard Copley and for the first time a Bursar, Mrs J. S. Evers, was appointed. The Educational Centres Association (ECA, formerly ESA until 1946) was also now examining its role in funding Swarthmore and had decided to withdraw support in favour of financing new centres elsewhere. For the time being at least the City was prepared to make up the difference and now provided two thirds of the Centre's income. In 1966–67 funding problems were worsened by the Labour government's guidance to local authorities to revise radically their fee structure. Swarthmore was forced to *double* its fees and as a consequence student numbers dropped by 10% but, ironically, revenue increased substantially and annual income grew to nearly £14,000. Swarthmore's autonomy appeared increasingly compromised by this dependent relationship to the LEA and it was obliged to see itself as an element of the City's broader adult education programme as well as holding on to its traditional independence. Riding these two horses, it could be argued, was profoundly to unsettle both the new Warden and a number of his successors. By the following year the new relationship directly affected the use of premises and length of term, which had to be shortened. Swarthmore was now asked to cooperate with neighbouring Park Lane College and Jacob Kramer Colleges by opening rooms to its overspill students during the day. This was not necessarily burdensome as it made good use of unused capacity and the introduction of young people rejuvenated the atmosphere – and future membership. Swarthmore of course was by now a significant property owner but the buildings needed repairing and renovation and a new appeal for £25,000 was launched. Much faith was placed in the convening of Lord Russell's committee on Adult Education by the government in 1968 and many felt a new era was approaching in which the measly 6% of the national educational budget allotted to adult education might be substantially increased. It was a long wait however and (as always) a false dawn; Russell didn't report until 1973 and then was ignored by the incoming Tory government.

But the partnership with the WEA for the provision of 'serious studies' was flourishing. Harry Newton[1] was appointed as the new WEA Tutor Organiser for Swarthmore and he worked closely with Richard Copley on programme planning and cooperating with the newly set-up Radio Leeds. The magic of broadcasting seemed to offer the potential for a whole new constituency of students, much as the excitement around the proposed 'University of the Air', then emanating from adult education and government circles, was suggesting. Energetic debates were held in Swarthmore about how it might contribute – and some members even remembered the radio broadcasts in the 1930s (see Chapter 2). These were heady times when doors were being burst open throughout education including, in a rather dramatic fashion, up the road at Leeds University, where the students had occupied the administrative buildings and were holding 24 hour seminars on the evils of capitalism, the joys of socialism, unlimited cannabis and free love. In the warm summer of 1968, revolution was, if not just in the air, then certainly on the airwaves.

The fabric also underwent changes. Despite their best efforts, the Students' Committee had been able to offer only a small coffee- and tea-making area in the basement, but in the era of the coffee bar as the new choice meeting place for young people, it was clearly not enough. The basement anyway was being adapted for pottery work and a second kiln was bought in 1966 to cope with student demand and higher quality work. So the Students' Committee now created a small refreshment area upstairs on the ground floor (roughly where it still is) and had bought curtains and a cash register to make it official – even the need for that most modern of appliances, a fridge, was discussed. The basement also housed a small second-hand book shop for fund-raising, constantly restocked by donations from students. Other signs of the new educational times included the purchase of a television, labs for language work and a printing press. A new appeal was launched in 1969 for £25,000 to renovate the fabric of numbers 3, 4 and 5 Woodhouse Square and to incorporate numbers 6 and 7, newly leased to Swarthmore by the City Council.

## Unleashing Creativity

The language programme still had the largest share of provision at about a third of the total 110 classes at its height in 1968–69. These were mainly German, Italian, French, Spanish and Russian, but Esperanto no longer attracted enough students to make up a class. Martha Steinitz's health began to fail and increasingly her place was taken by her sister Hedwig and Hansi Barrett, with Miss Jungmann taking classes in German Literature. Dr Mendel and Mrs Thorne taught French while Miss Tomasini now taught in the region of six Italian classes weekly. Sadly, Martha Steinitz died in 1969 and a Memorial Fund was set up in her name to send students on educational visits abroad. The huge response, displayed in the letters of donation received by the Warden, testified to the place she held in Swarthmore's affection. (The fund shortly allowed an outstanding but impoverished student of German, Harold Kettlewell, to spend two weeks in Vienna.) A living link to Swarthmore's early days was broken but it was also clear that the new times had not been to Miss Steinitz's taste. The new Arts Council exhibitions on display at Swarthmore, which included nudity, had latterly evoked her (considerable) wrath and she wrote in no uncertain terms to the Director claiming that such exhibitions brought the Arts Council and Swarthmore into disrepute. Not every one agreed, including the Warden, and sides were taken (Brian Thompson, private communication, 2008).

Social studies in cooperation with WEA and the University, now occupied almost a quarter of the programme. They took on a keen radical edge with a pioneering course by Pat Calder and Chris Duke on Chapeltown – the Study of an Urban Community, which engaged members of the community in action research. Maureen Baker followed up with a highly challenging course on Community and Race, signifying Swarthmore's recharged commitment to studying

### She taught German for nearly 40 years

The death has occurred of Miss Martha Steinitz, who for nearly 40 years taught German at the Swarthmore Educational Centre, Leeds. She was 77.

Miss Steinitz, of Estcourt Avenue, Leeds, was made an honorary graduate of Leeds University for her work with adult students.

She lectured on art history for many years, and organised an annual Sommerfest of Music and Poetry. Her death took place just as she was completing her last term's work before retirement.

She is survived by an elder sister.

Pottery workshop, 1960s

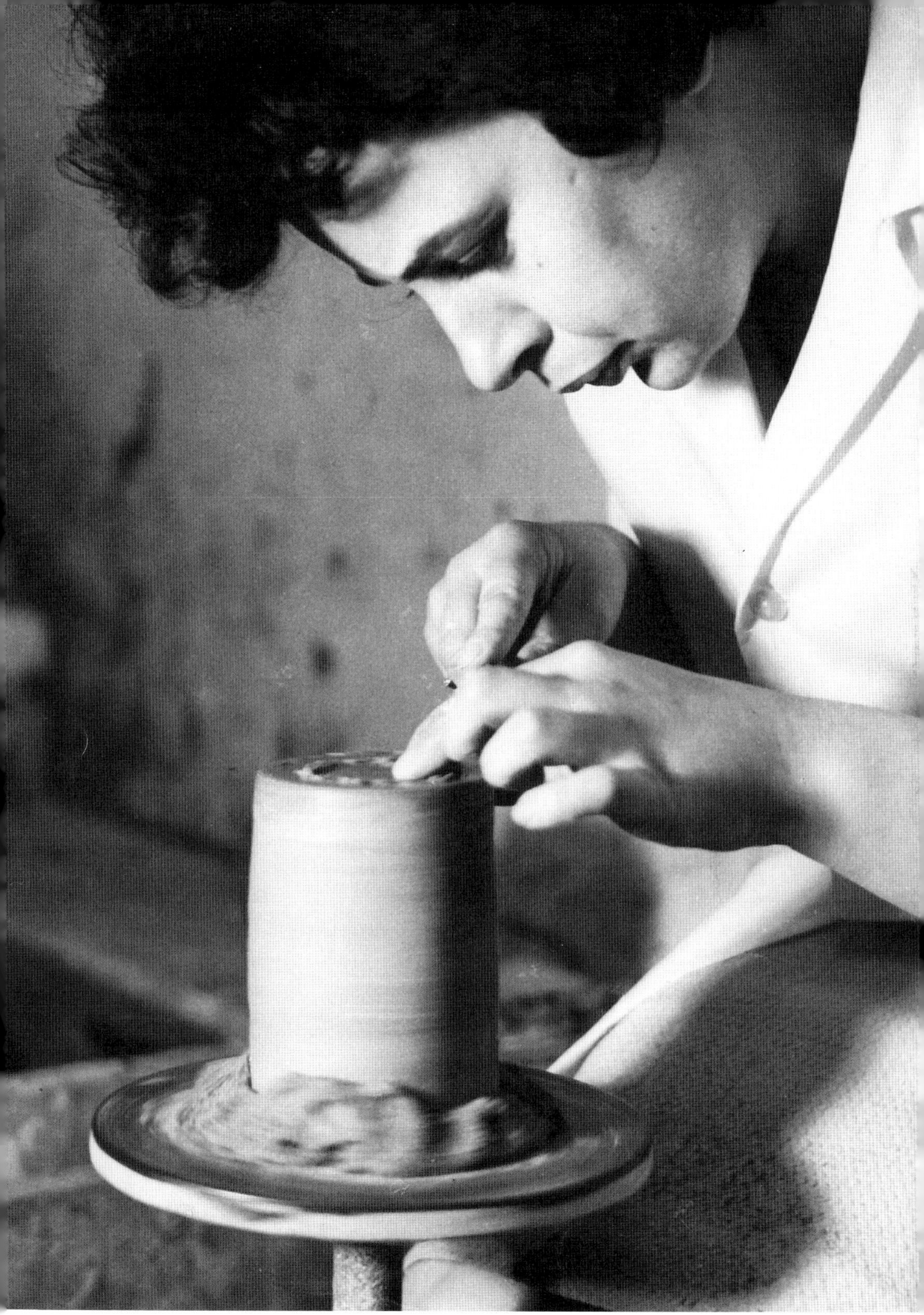

contemporary social issues. A lecturer from York University, Adrian Leftwitch, who had been imprisoned in South Africa for his opposition to the apartheid regime, taught a class on Marxism. The burgeoning civil rights movement in the USA was also brought vividly home to Leeds by Frank Howard, who had himself been an activist in Alabama and had witnessed white racism at first hand, in a course called Freedom in America. But perhaps the first class in Leeds to express the radical new interest in 'Women's Studies' brought about the by the Women's Movement was Jackie Wooton's course on Women: the Second Sex? Such inspired programming again showed how quickly Swarthmore, as a student democracy, could respond to emergent social issues. Other courses, largely on the WEA programme, indicating sharpened social awareness included Law and the Citizen, People and Planning and Educational Issues, Local Government by Bill Pritchard and Care in the Community by Leeds Council for Social Services. Classes in Third World Political Change, Modern China, and Latin America by Phil Ralph, the new WEA Tutor Organiser, augmented Swarthmore's internationalist concerns and what was to become an enduring theme, Britain and the Common Market. Swarthmore broke new ground by offering an Introduction to Social Science and Literature for students intending to take up distance learning courses at the newly launched Open University (as the 'University of the Air' had now become).

Even the science classes caught the pioneering mood with another first, the Natural History of the City taught by Mark Seaward, which – to the bewilderment of more established figures – had class members on their hands and knees grubbing up bits of flora between Leeds city-centre paving stones. Man in Space by Dr Jakeways also breathed the rarefied atmosphere of American moon landings and Russian cosmonauts, when it seemed space really was the final frontier, while a class on the Double Helix by Simon Baumberg had people in bars (after the class) excitedly talking about DNA.

New classes on Experimental Music and Jazz Appreciation too added to the atmosphere. Arts provision generally grew in strength with courses on drama, film and photography. Martin Banham from the University's Theatre Studies department took course members to the theatre and Alec Baron campaigned for a regional playhouse to be based in Leeds (which was to become the West Yorkshire Playhouse). Clifford Laycock and Jennifer Megson offered Theatre Workshop courses for practitioners. Les Reyner introduced members to the kind of European art films, like *Zazi dans le Metro*, not shown in commercial cinemas, and there was a practical course on film-making by Shirley Bork. The serious study of the arts was of course well-maintained in this heady atmosphere with courses on York Festival Music, English Church Music and the Greek Heritage, Literary Criticism by Walter Stein and Literature and Society by Roy Shaw, while historical work continued with classes in Industrial Archaeology by Richard Copley. Even here though the age could not be denied and a course on Four Revolutionary Figures by Gordon Hainsworth studied Cromwell, Robespierre, Lenin and somewhat surprisingly, Hitler.

Although languages were the long-term bedrock of Swarthmore's provision, they were closely followed in popularity by the practical arts and crafts and the Centre's reputation had justly grown in the post-war decades, as we have seen. With the second kiln in place, pottery classes taught by Stan Stemp and Pam Rex grew substantially, the Centre offering five courses for beginners alone by the mid-1960s. Potters would labour long and hard at the often not so yielding clay but those pieces not deemed fit for completion were then ritually smashed in what Thompson called a 'triage' of destruction – much fine work however resulted. Painting classes had become well-established and diversified with around eight courses in portrait, 'Big' painting, life, model painting and print-making. Tutors regularly took classes out at weekends to study nature and landscape, with weekends at Grantley Hall.

Still there was a problem in that most of the classes took place at night and Council discussed how to use the premises more effectively during the day. Thompson came up with the proposal for afternoon classes targeted at women with children with a crèche to be provided – probably the first in Leeds for educational purposes. At its height in the late 1960s, over 30 afternoon courses were offered, taking in the full swathe of Swarthmore's provision, and they proved very popular. It was possible to study no less than seven languages, sociology, public speaking, theatre design, women's issues, flower arranging, gardening, creative writing, art, dance and embroidery. The Centre also announced a full summer programme which took the chance of offering tasters for the Autumn programme, while allowing the language classes to continue into the holidays. A new departure was the five-day courses, running from 6–9 pm, offering the opportunity to 'cram a big experience into a short time span'. Perhaps the most ambitious was a course in sculpture in which the students were asked to produce a relief mural for Swarthmore.

### Brian Thompson

Warden 196-1973. A grammar school boy from Waltham Cross, after a spell of National Service in Bradford and Bury St Edmunds, Thompson applied to Cambridge from a NAAFI hut, he claims, but his place was deferred for a two-year stint as a subaltern in Kenya, unhappily attempting to suppress the Mau Mau, one of his charges being Idi Amin. He graduated from Trinity College, Cambridge, as a mature student, with a degree in English in 1957 and after a speckled early career became an established playwright and biographer, his two recent volumes of autobiographical memoirs, 'Keeping Mum' (2006) and 'Clever Girl' (2007) receiving critical acclaim for their astute combination of emotional frankness and bald humour. His memoirs reveal an unhappy childhood, suffering from punitive parents. His third volume of memoirs, which will reveal more of his time at Swarthmore, is awaited with baited breath.

Brian Thompson's greatest success was the promotion of Creative Writing, building on the groundwork of his predecessor, Brian Stapleton, and the undoubted talents of Bill Price Turner. He drew in a range of poets including George Kendrick, David MacAndrew, Pete Morgan, and the then Gregory Fellow, Martin Bell. Another published poet, Muriel Berry, became a long term and much admired tutor into the 1980s and Thompson himself taught many classes. Novel writing flourished and Swarthmore fostered new talent. Margaret Jones, for example, was awarded best first novel of 1968 award by *The Daily Telegraph* for *The Day they Put Humpty Together Again* (Collins, 1968). Another outstanding novel was *As I was Going to St Ives* by Elsie Nokes, (whose Foreword praised Bill Price Turner for his inspiration). Elizabeth North published her outstanding work *The Least and Vilest Things* (Gollancz, 1971), the first of her nine novels, which sounded a clarion call for women to throw off their chains: 'I have decided I may become an emergent woman', announced its heroine Hannah Green, after twelve earthbound years of marriage. Significantly, not only did this reflect the burgeoning 'Second Wave Feminism' about to transform women's lives in the 1970s but also enduring continuity with the late-nineteenth century wave of feminist writing that nourished suffragism[2].

### The Piper's Tune

Despite all this creativity and surfing the zeitgeist (or perhaps because of it) Swarthmore's status was increasingly uncertain and some among the City fathers demanded greater accountability for their substantial financial stake in the Centre. A Working Party was set up in February 1973 with representatives from all the partners including the University, WEA, LEA, Quakers, HMI, and Educational Centres Association together with Brian Thompson, Richard Copley and delegates from the Council. Its brief was, ominously, 'to consider the future role of Swarthmore as an adult education centre'. Despite its path-breaking

Dance class, 1960s

provision, it did not fit the *conventional* pattern of adult education provision and so a strong case had to be put forward for its distinctiveness. The Working Party's report stressed the diversity of provision under one roof and the possibilities of cross-fertilization (much as Stapleton had earlier argued). It pointed to the variety of levels of learning, allowing for what now is called 'progression' (but then by the more picturesque phrasing of a 'place of beginnings and continuings'). Its informal atmosphere and community spirit, democratic management and daytime provision were also justly celebrated.

All this was an impressive defence of Swarthmore's uniqueness but in the end it came down to basics – where was the brass to come from? The City was prepared to stump up but no longer on the old formula of set grants, reflecting the number of classes provided (too many in some opinions) and deficit funding. Their new proposal was for the Wardens' salaries to be protected but the rest of the authority's grant to be derived from 'capitation' (bums on seats) with the implication there was going to have to be some restraint in provision. Because, under this formula, income would fall in real terms, there would be a strong temptation for Swarthmore to provide only money-making classes and lose the more experimental or minority-interest classes. The report proposed a new partnership to be made between Swarthmore and the City to serve the whole of Leeds – although how this differed from what existed, except in formalities, was hard to see. Perhaps the point was that the City would now be seen as a major 'partner', while Swarthmore's independence and democratic control would remain. The upshot was that, in collaboration with the other partners, Swarthmore would now have to submit estimates for its planned provision and not rely on previous custom and practice. These would then be audited to ensure that expenditure matched estimates. A new financial era had dawned and the piper was, if not actually calling the tune, at least setting the tempo. Despite successfully piloting the report through some stormy seas, in which it is reliably reported feelings ran high, Brian Thompson decided it was time to move on and resume his interrupted vocation as a writer.

Thus over the decade, due to the government's new funding regulations, Swarthmore had been obliged to move decisively into the orbit of Leeds LEA, so what was once a supported relationship became increasingly one of subordination to external financial imperatives. It was of course a 'partnership', but one in which there were juniors and seniors. At the same time the Centre blossomed into a considerable Arts Centre, offering a unique array of practical and academic courses, always backed by a critical engagement with social concerns. Its innovatory approach to the needs of its members, especially women, its reaching out to excluded groups, informal teaching strategies and internationalist perspective gave it an enviable national reputation, celebrated as we shall see in the next chapter, at the highest levels.

Swarthmore Nursery,
September 1963

## Notes

[1] Harry Newton, a former communist who left the party in 1956 after the Soviet Union invaded Hungary, was a much loved tutor in the WEA and later at Fircroft College and highly regarded in his work for the trade unions under the WETUC scheme of industrial education. But Harry may not have been all that he seemed and he was exposed as an agent in the 1980s by MI5 whistleblower, Cathy Massiter, who claimed she was his 'Controller' and that he had been working for MI5 since the late 1950s. Harry's disillusion with communism had turned him into a born-again Christian and he was recruited to spy on the activities of CND, including his old comrade, Edward Thompson, who also taught occasionally at Swarthmore and who had just completed his classic social history *The Making of the English Working Class* (based very much on his adult education classes in the West Riding). Later, in the run-up to the 1984 Miners Strike, MI5 tried to get Harry to spy on Arthur Scargill and the NUM at their Barnsley headquarters but he died. Scargill, who had been one his students in the Miner's day release classes at Leeds University's Adult Education Department was rather bemused by the allegations, telling Seamus Milne, 'I regarded him as a very dedicated and loyal member of the movement' (Milne, 2004). Harry was remembered with great affection by colleagues and friends in the pages of the *Guardian*. H. D. Beeby of St Andrews Missionary Hall College in Selly Oak for example wrote: 'To those of us who knew and loved Harry and respected both his communist and Christian convictions, this is information [Massiter's revelations] that beggars language. Words such as "bizarre", "impossible", "incredible" are not adequate' (*Guardian* Letters page 2 March 1985). Edward Thompson, himself, in the same pages also expressed measured incredulity: 'I also knew Harry Newton on and off for 30 years in the adult education and other movements. He was an unlikely agent. But then as an historian of such things [...] I know that agents always are unlikely persons' (Ibid; see also John Saville (2003) *Memoirs from the Left*, London; Merlin Press, pp124–127).

[2] Perhaps not surprisingly, an interesting but now largely ignored novel of this period was by none other than Isabella Ford, a Quaker member of the original Swarthmore Council. Her novel *On the Threshold* (1895) as June Hannam notes: 'explored the dilemmas faced by young middle-class women who enjoyed greater personal freedoms than their mothers but were still confined by social expectations and conventions' (Hannam 1989:87) *Plus ça change*.

Front cover and inside pages from the 1959-60 Swarthmore Winter Syllabus

**CHAPTER 6**

# Social Purpose, Community Action and the Arts, 1973–1993

There was good reason to believe that the new settlement with the City could, so long as Swarthmore kept its nose clean, usher in a period of stability. Despite the reluctance of the new Conservative government to implement the Russell Report, it was felt that the adult education world had received public reassurance that the work it was doing was valued, especially if a firm commitment could be set for social concerns. Indeed Fred Sedgwick, the WEA Yorkshire North District Secretary, who had largely authored the WEA's submission, thought that the WEA could return to the 'unfinished business' of education for the underprivileged. A flurry of new appointments was made. Paul Roche, the assistant Warden had taken over temporarily on Brian Thompson's departure but in September 1974 Martin Russell was appointed Warden. His tenure of nineteen years was to be the longest served, during which time the Centre changed dramatically. The core elements of language teaching remained while its Arts Centre potential was consolidated, resulting in new Art Studios, an enlarged pottery studio, a jewellery studio and by 1990 a new purpose-built hall for dance and drama. But increasingly the Centre became the place of reference for a much wider group of cultural and campaigning organisations, which by the 1990s had grown to over 60 groups, ranging from Swarthmore birdwatchers to Gay Rights campaigners. Russell's open-door approach to self-organising groups was applied to the Centre's own programme planning, where a small but significant proportion of the budget was reserved for trying out new ideas. This meant that any new proposal that fitted the ethos of the Centre was guaranteed a hearing by the Programme Planning Committee and, if viable, a space on the programme. This resulted in many innovative (occasionally whacky) courses and experimental directions. Some were passed on to the WEA or University if they seemed more appropriate to these partner providers.

Members were given a much bigger say in how the Centre was run and information increased exponentially – bulletins, newsletters, appeals and leaflets poured out of the effervescing Roneo machines (this was before photocopying) and onto notice boards and coffee tables. Members were now regularly asked their opinions and were press-ganged to serve on Swarthmore's committees. These now included a successor to the Students' Committee, the House Committee, which was at the heart of the Centre. It ran the coffee bar, the crèche and playgroup, decorated these areas and organised social events, all on a voluntary basis, with their own separate financial account. Brian Thompson had initiated a class representatives' committee, which was encouraged to bring suggestions and complaints to the Warden. In addition to this long-standing tradition of student democracy, Russell proposed a Programme Planning Board and by the end of the 1980s an Equal Opportunities Committee. As well as his admiration for Swarthmore's voluntarism, Russell was moved by the work of the great Brazilian educator Paulo Freire whose *Pedagogy of the Oppressed* had been recently translated into English and by the Russian 'deschooler' Ivan Illich. All cloth kits, woolly jumpers and bad hair, one long-standing member recalled, but Swarthmore had a vibrancy unmatched in the north.

The relationship with the WEA was consolidated by the appointment of another Tutor Organiser for Swarthmore in 1975, the author of this history, whose job it was to work with the Leeds branch to coordinate the WEA and Leeds University Joint Committee programmes of liberal adult education. Sadly, Fred Sedgwick who was a great WEA pioneer of 'social purpose' education had to have a cancerous leg amputated in 1974 and never recovered full health. In 1976 he retired and died a few months later to be replaced by John Croft, a former Ruskin student and trade union organiser. The government intimated that 'Russell-type' work (work with the 'disadvantaged') might be favourably viewed if quantified plans could be put forward, but in the event no new funding was made available. Sedgwick was anyway worried that the WEA might be drawn into a kind of social service 'rescue' work rather than the provision of liberal adult education for working people for which it was established in 1903. Although sceptical, he handed me Tom Lovett's (now seminal) book *Adult education, community development and the working class* (1975) which he thought might suggest new directions, but for him it was quite a distance from the days when the WEA in

Yorkshire would measure educational success by how many of its members served on public bodies and represented working people in local and national government. It was as if the larger political ambitions of working-class education had now been relegated to something called 'community education'. As the leading historian of Modern British Adult education Roger Fieldhouse (then Academic Adviser for Tutorial Classes in the Leeds Adult Education Department) noted at the time: 'we should avoid being forced into the role of a cheap, amateur and inexpert social service. That is not our function and I don't think we would be particularly good at it if we tried to do it' (quoted in Croft, 2002: 49).

### Russell Work

Despite misgivings, the atmosphere of 'Russell Work' predominated. Many saw it as an opportunity to return adult education to a more socially committed kind of learning and ease it away from the misfired idea of the previous decade, 'leisure' education. The University increased its presence at Swarthmore, both through the traditional Joint Committee evening classes and day-time courses for social workers on the part-time Diploma in Social Work course, run by Mark Beeson. Similarly with the advent of the Labour government and its funding for trade union education in the late 1970s, the WEA increased its day-time provision at Swarthmore by providing courses for shop stewards and Health and Safety representatives on the TUC day release scheme, organised by another WEA Tutor Organiser, Philip Ralph and myself. Under Martin Russell, Swarthmore grasped the new era with both hands and initiated a variety of projects aimed at those with no or little experience of post-school education and in particular those suffering the consequences of economic recession. These ranged from literacy courses, classes for the unemployed, work with the disabled, outreach work with excluded groups including Asian women and one of the first Higher Education 'Access' schemes (with Leeds Polytechnic) called 'Fresh Starts'. A source of much brow-wrinkling was the question of whether examination qualifications should be introduced, a major break with tradition. A heated Council meeting decided to introduce exams for the short-lived Home Study project but it forced the resignation of a number of long-standing members in disagreement, including Alderman Alf Tallant (whose father had been a founder of the Leeds WEA branch in 1907 and a passionate supporter of Swarthmore).

Nevertheless GCSE courses were introduced and stayed on the programme from the middle-1980s largely in response to student requests from the Second Chance and Fresh Start programmes and increased demands from the City Council to target specific needs.

Literacy, or rather illiteracy, had been flagged up nationally as an appalling indictment of a wealthy industrial nation, with research showing that something like one in four of adults still had a reading age of below 10 years and that an intolerably high proportion of unskilled workers were simply unable to read at all. Leeds City Council launched a city-wide scheme for training voluntary teachers to work with illiteracy in 1975. Swarthmore promptly signed up to this and dedicated a room two evenings a week for training sessions. Notices in the windows and word of mouth alerted those who might know people with reading problems that here was a centre to which they might come for advice and indeed many came through the doors. (Many others mistook it for the Night Shelter for the Homeless at St George's Crypt across the foot bridge and after whiling away an hour or three in the coffee bar were gently led in the right direction.) Voluntary tutors were trained and groups met at the centre, finding it a welcoming and hospitable place, far removed from the forbidding schoolrooms and practices of their youth.

The biggest scourge of the age was of course unemployment, growing uncomfortably under the Labour government during the late-1970s. It reached epidemic proportions by the early eighties under Mrs Thatcher's fundamentalist Toryism, which scythed away great swathes of Leeds's manufacturing base and cut social services to the bone. However, a curious side effect was that the Tory government's attempt to ameliorate the most visible effects of unemployment unexpectedly created new sources of funding. Swarthmore was quickly aware of the potential which might reduce its dependence on the LEA and responded in a variety of imaginative ways, beginning with housing a Youth Opportunities Programme (YOPS) run by a WEA tutor, Lee Comer. Lee Comer was one of the leaders of the new wave of feminist writers in Britain having recently published her seminal work *Wedlocked Women* (1974). Feminism was now very much on the agenda at Swarthmore and a range of courses, as we shall see, later reflected this new militant consciousness. An unemployment advice centre was initiated in 1983, which led perhaps to its most ambitious project, the 'Second Chance to Learn' programme. Running for the next six years, this programme was funded by the Manpower Services Commission (MSC) under the Voluntary Projects Programme (VPP) as a Basic Education programme for unemployed adults. Initially six courses were provided, three 'Starter' courses for learning skills in maths, English and communications and three in Science and Technology, covering physics, electronics and computing – and more maths, the first intake attracting around 43 students. The courses were supervised by Jim Billingham and then Val Finnigan with an ever changing team of part time tutors – the MSC's part-time hours and rates of pay never enough to guarantee stability (AR 1982–83). It continued to grow through the 1980s claiming 55% 'positive progression' – as the MSC's bureaucratic terminology described finding a job. As Val Finnigan noted in her 1986 report to Swarthmore: 'It is a particular irony we live with that our success in terms of recruitment is because there are so many people going through the misery of unemployment' (AR 1985–86). At its height the Second Chance scheme offered over 20 classes weekly for over 100 unemployed adults and overall around 1500 people benefited before its funding was abruptly cut in 1989. For most it was their first experience of education since leaving school, offering a pathway into further education and paid work. Beyond those quantifiable successes it was hard to estimate the broader value of the scheme, which raised the abilities and self-esteem of many for whom unemployment might have meant the end of hope.

A further response to the growing tide of unemployment was the 'Get it Together' scheme organised jointly with Geoff Hill at Voluntary Action Leeds (VAL), funded by NIACE REPLAN (don't ask) and run by Maggie Jones for two years, 1987–89. Noted for her energy and imagination, Maggie Jones explored the potential for community-based learning in Seacroft and Burley, two of Leeds's very deprived areas. Eight different community learning initiatives were set up in the two areas offering welfare advice, parenting groups, community newspapers, women's groups including for the first time, Asian women's groups – a delighted member of the one of the Burley Asian women's group reported back to Swarthmore: 'I never realised before – all the things I can do! My husband thinks I am stupid – now I can show him he has made a big mistake' (AR 1988–89: 14). The scheme showed what inroads could be

Firing up the outside kiln, 1970s

made into communities traditionally shy of adult education with just a modest grant and a committed organiser. Equally, it all too well demonstrated the frustration of short-term funding, which could be terminated just when headway was being made.

Swarthmore became home to the bewilderingly acronymned TOWCAS (The Out of Work Counselling and Advice Service) which had its origins in the Unemployment Advice Centre referred to above. This was a long-standing group of around 20 activists, founded in 1983 with a small grant from Leeds City Council. It was one of the first groups of its kind in Leeds and it spurred Leeds Trades Council to set up its own unemployment centre, TUCRIC (Trade Union and Community Resource and Information Centre). TOWCAS had a small office for advice but was probably best known for its city-wide newssheet and its booklet 'Survival on the Dole'. There was even a video produced, called 'Down the Road', directed by and starring unemployed members. Although it offered education classes funded by the University and the WEA, in things like photography, they were only intermittently successful. However, the experience gave rise to Swarthmore establishing its own Welfare Rights project in 1988 funded by Leeds Society of Friends, reawakening the old Quaker links. Janice Fife, the Welfare Rights worker employed on the project, described the service as offering advice on appeals for benefits, negotiating with loan companies and fuel boards, and writing to local charities for support which, as entitlement to benefit decreased, was increasingly necessary.

With all this activity the walls were once again bulging and the floors creaking. It was decided to replace the old hall (funded by Bernard Lyons in the 1950s) in 1983. The financial confidence Swarthmore had gained in bidding for MSC grants to tackle the effects of unemployment, led it to put in a bid for a self-build project using unemployed workers. Indeed it was chance remark from an MSC inspector that started the ball rolling (AR 1982–83). It was a very bold idea and, happily, not quite fatal (see below). The project was to build a much enlarged brick hall to replace the previous concrete and metal tie structure with a dedicated dance and drama space and a new art studio. The MSC approved Swarthmore's application for £214,000 in January 1983 but £100,000 had to be raised from elsewhere to cover materials, since the MSC grant only covered labour. Leeds City Council provided £40,000 from its capital grants allocation and supported Swarthmore's application to the Inner Cities Fund (set up by Michael Heseltine). Once again its vigorous membership came up with a fertile range of fund raising projects and the £100,000 was found.

Swarthmore was to manage the build, using unemployed workers and a team of architects and surveyors. Russell's own gripping account of the final moments of the old hall shows just how knife-edge the project was:

> *I regard it as a miracle that we completed this project without killing anyone and ended up with a building which shows every sign of not collapsing. Of the 22 men employed only four of them had any real building skills training. The plumber, who was more than a little enthusiastic about Mr Tetley's products, had to be paid as late as possible on the Thursday pay-day, because as soon as he was paid he disappeared to the pub and often was not seen again till Monday morning. Miraculously we managed to recruit two excellent bricklayers onto the team. Without them the project and the building would have collapsed. And finally the site manager, had had quite a lot of experience as a site manager, but was an Irish maverick who played drums in an Irish folk group and was not an enthusiast for rules, regulations and precise accounting. The most alarming moment in the whole project was when the team had taken the roof off the hall, leaving the walls standing, [comprising] a large rectangle of concrete pillars 12 feet high, with concrete slats inserted between the pillars to form the walls. The structure was clearly held in place by a tie bar that ran round the top of the pillars. It was decided that in order to tackle demolition of the walls, the tie bar would have to be severed and removed, then the concrete slats could be lifted out. I happened to be looking out of my office window at the potentially fatal moment. The whole building team was standing inside the square shell of the building. One worker was up a stepladder at one corner of the building sawing through something that was clearly felt to be important. He finished sawing, gave a thumbs up sign and was just turning to descend the ladder when, from the point where he had sawn, the walls of the hall elegantly peeled away and fell outwards in a fanlike ripple. Where there had been walls moments before, there was now just a*

*huge cloud of dust, a pile of rubble in the road and backyard, and a group of bewildered workers not believing what they had just witnessed. It was all over in a few seconds.*
(Martin Russell, personal communication, 2008)

In another, much publicised, Gothic interlude, a human skeleton found while digging out the foundations for the new hall eventually turned out merely to have gone walkabout from its usual home in the Art Studio resource cupboard, much to the amusement of the resident sculptor[1]. The hall was opened by Prof Bernard Jennings (President of the WEA) on 25th May 1985, with a dedication to the challenging and visionary educational work Swarthmore had embodied in its three quarters of a century, unaware perhaps of just how close to the edge of its comfort zone it had just strayed.

### Fresh Starts

Another product of the creative thinking of this period was the path-breaking Fresh Start programme. One of the earliest initiatives of what came to be called the 'Access movement' in the late 1970s, Fresh Starts was aimed at adults who had missed out on further or higher education and who had little or no education since leaving school. It provided a structured return-to-learning programme in an informal environment with counselling and tutorial support, a crèche and a playgroup. Few centres in the country could match this kind of support for mature students and it provided a benchmark for access provision. At its height, Fresh Starts offered four levels of courses: a Basic Course for absolute beginners of one full day a week; a Gateway Course which was introductory for those with more experience; the Foundation Course of two full days a week for those who had come through the first two or were already more confident; finally there was a Continuation Course for the who had passed through Foundation and wanted to pursue studies in greater depth. The courses ran for thirty weeks over three terms, or twenty two in the case of the Continuation course, 9.30–3.00 costing £35 for the Foundation Course and £20 for the others – extraordinarily modest by today's standards even if such courses existed.

The WEA was fully engaged with this programme and contributed tutors in English, Sociology, Philosophy and History. An informal arrangement with Leeds Polytechnic

(Leeds Metropolitan University) was made to admit recommended students into degree programmes in lieu of A levels, making it a highly effective paradigm of informal partnership, while others progressed into Further and Higher Education. Much of the success of the programme was down to the skill, warmth and dedication of Pamela Cole who became its Tutor Organiser. She recounts in one Annual Report how she took students to see a performance of *Educating Rita* at the West Yorkshire Playhouse and then cheekily asked its author Willy Russell to talk to her own class of Ritas, which he did with relish. Perhaps, not surprisingly, most Fresh Start students were women, whose educational prospects had been eclipsed by a combination of families, financial dependence, low self-esteem or unhelpful partners. For many the courses were a revelation of what they could achieve given the chance. Word came back from grateful students of careers in nursing, acting and social services and far personal horizons visited. Sue Branney took over when Pam Cole moved on and the success of the programme stimulated Leeds University's Adult and Continuing Education Department to begin its own Women's Access provision, which Jean Gardiner was appointed to lead. Arising to an extent from the pastoral experience of Fresh Starts, one final innovation advanced by the fertile Programme Planning Board, was in Personal Effectiveness and Counselling Skills, which were introduced in the late 1980s. Counselling Skills in particular took off and soon the centre was running a series of major courses at Diploma level under the direction of Hazel Hobbs.

## Social Entrepreneurialism

It could be well argued that all this was possible because of the combination of inspired leadership, voluntary enthusiasm, open networks, supportive institutional frameworks and, in the best sense, the *entrepreneurial* vitality that Swarthmore embodied. Indeed it was kind of 'social entrepreneurialism' *avant le lettre* (the sociologist Michael Young invented the term in the 1990s) in which the profits were ploughed back into the community chest rather than the private purse. For Swarthmore the milk cow that provided much of the cash for these innovatory projects was its English for Foreign Students (EFS) programme which ran from 1977-1983. These were courses in which foreign nationals paid substantial fees to learn English in Britain. Originally, while the nearby Park Lane College offered a substantial range of day-time opportunities,

Swarthmore offered just one evening course. When Park Lane could no longer respond to increased demand, Swarthmore gladly took up the slack, expanding to five full-time day courses. According to Russell, the income from this provision enabled Swarthmore to make a number of crucial appointments. The first was a part time Assistant Warden to replace the one that had mysteriously disappeared between Russell's interview in 1974 and his taking up the post. It contributed to Pamela Cole's position as Fresh Start organiser and an EFS organiser, as well as providing equipment and refurbishment of the centre.

Interestingly, this could be seen as a renewal of Swarthmore's inter-war internationalism, when English for Foreign students was first introduced – mainly for Jewish refugees from Nazism (see Chapter 2). Many students were refugees from oppressive Middle Eastern governments and the Iran/Iraq War, waged fruitlessly (despite Anglo-American backing for the subsequently demonised Saddam Hussein) throughout the period. But although Swarthmore did indeed bring its own inimitable colouring to the provision, it was an area of work which was welcomed largely because of its income-producing potential.

The income from this source inevitably came to an end, due to the Thatcher government's imposition of minimum fees of around £1,500 for international students. This more or less killed off the golden goose. It was capped by the tragic shooting of WPC Yvonne Fletcher outside the Libyan Embassy in April 1984. Swarthmore was owed £3,000 by the Libyans in student fees, which were never paid. Swarthmore's attempt to get round these measures by setting up the Leeds Independent Language Trust, came too late and EFS disappeared from the programme the following year.

Other income came from Swarthmore's decision in 1975 to buy number 2 Woodhouse Square, which had been used for many years as a store for architectural salvage, for the sum of £12,000. The additional space acquired allowed it to resite the crèche in a bigger room in the main building with nappy-changing facilities, while the ground floor was subsequently let to an educationally sympathetic body, working with ethnic minorities, West Yorkshire Language Link. One final example of Swarthmore's commitment to social purpose was its partnership with the Sharing Care project in providing day-time classes for those with learning disabilities, which included a pioneering dance class, and continue to the present day.

## Arts Fellowships, Politics and Feminism

There could be no doubt about Swarthmore's serious commitment to challenging educational deprivation in these schemes, which were amongst the most imaginative in the country and attracted widespread approval. However they did not detract from its long term commitment to Arts education and its growing function as an Arts Centre. In many ways they actually enhanced it as the social relevance of creative work was increasingly fore-grounded.

The most important of Russell's innovations was his introduction of a series Arts Fellowships through a successful bid to Yorkshire Arts Association. Artists in Residence funded by the grants included a painter, Andrew Turner; potters, Dennis Farrell and Sue King (whose ceramic mural in the coffee-bar is now sadly boarded over); a sculptor, Lesley Yendell and a weaver, Brigitte Gibbon whose communal 'Weave-In' produced an 8' x 4' hanging for the coffee bar. Elizabeth North, herself a graduate of Swarthmore's creative writing classes in the 1960s (see last chapter) gained a Fellowship and organised a very successful national creative writing competition. The prize winning entries were published in Swarthmore Writers-One (1984) which she edited and introduced. There was also a playwright, Chris Hawes, one of whose students, Ron Pearson, won the BBC Playwriting competition in 1986 with a prize of £4,500 and his hour and a half play was performed on prime time TV. Barbara Roberts won a first prize in a *Woman's Own* national competition for short stories (AR 1985/86).

In Russell's view these Fellowships made a major contribution to the careers of the artists concerned and the creative life of the centre not only in stimulating individuals but by enabling related course programmes, such as that in Art History by Shirley Moreno. The freewheeling nature of these fellowships was, however, curtailed when in the late 1980s, Yorkshire Arts decided to replace funding for practising artists with 'targeted' work, involving the appointment of *animateurs* to stimulate arts activity amongst minority groups. There followed two appointments: an Arts worker for black communities in Leeds, Cavell Brown, and a creative writing worker, Julie Hyam (known as Julie Ward ) who encouraged people with learning disabilities to tell their own stories. She encouraged some remarkable work, culminating in an exhibition and after funding was wound up, took the project forward herself to produce a booklet of graphic short stories based on students' work, *Not a Kid Anymore* (AR 1988–89).

The Arts thus remained at the centre of Swarthmore's life, maintaining the post-war growth and confirming its role as an Arts Centre. Talented tutors continued to energise students and a steady stream of exhibitions of painting and pottery both by students and visitors enlivened the coffee bar. One, a meditation on skinhead culture called *Lament of the Terraces*

*(Skinaphobia)* by performance artist, Michael Furbank, even caught the admiring attention of the *New Musical Express* (NME, 23.2.1980: 11). A significant educational advance was the introduction of the 'Extended Visual Arts Certificate' which enabled students over three or four years to develop a portfolio and record of work which was then authoritatively assessed. For many, this became a springboard into Art College and a higher education qualification. Alongside the new kiln and extension of the pottery studio, etching and screen printing were introduced. A jewellery studio and woodcarving area were built and a range of classes developed. These were largely pioneered by Jonathan Phillips, who personally built the Jewellery work benches and designed the workshop lay-out - a testament to the kind of voluntary input that the centre attracted at the time.

The sculpture studio was enlarged and improved and in 1985 a very fine new art studio was opened along with the hall. The dance programme, which while the hall was being re-built had met in venues outside Swarthmore, now had a permanent home. From the late 1970s Liz Normaschild had developed Contemporary Dance and this was complemented by classes in Yoga and T'ai Chi which quickly developed full programmes as the New Age drew on. Though no longer a prime feature of the programme as in the past, the drama group led by David Robertson continued to meet on Friday evenings and produced the Christmas pantomime.

Music provision grew substantially, adding classes in tin whistle and folk fiddle for example and a thirty-strong People's Choir. Jack Glover composed two oratorios, which were performed at the Centre to widespread acclaim. There was something special in the shape of the guitar classes given by Jonathan Phillips[2]. The WEA played its part by organising classes for the unemployed in how to form a rock band. These were led by Jon Langford of the legendary Mekons and Three Johns, then an art student in Leeds, and Tony Baker whose numerous New Country bands included Johnny Jumps the Bandwagon that played many a joyful fund-raising gig during the miners' strike in 1984–85. Baker's class, entitled 'I am Normal and I Dig Bert Weedon' was, of course, a great hit.

It's hard to conjure up the atmosphere around Swarthmore in these days. There was a continuous buzz of activity and excitement in innovation capped by serious political talk about the egregious Thatcher and her henchmen and the growing tide of unemployment and redundancy as 'uneconomic' industry collapsed and the dole queues grew. But by the late 1970s another threat was haunting the area, that of Peter Sutcliffe the 'Yorkshire Ripper' whose inhumane activities cast a shadow over the evening programme – one of his victims was attacked not half a mile away in Belle Vue Rd and another murdered in Alma Rd, Headingley. Notices warning women not go out alone were displayed, escorts offered and special taxi services were organised. Angry women marched on the local cinema and broke up the performance of a salacious film showing a woman being savagely attacked by a knife-wielding man. Feminism in Leeds may have taken on its particularly militant character as a result of these activities. The programme reflected this in such classes on Women's Self Defence taught by the wonderfully named Suzie Cannon and Assertiveness Training for Women by Em Edmondson. A range of feminist approaches to subjects by the WEA including anthropology, art history, literature, film studies and even, er, bicycle maintenance broke new ground. There were classes for men on childcare and what the new feminism had to say about masculinity (not about building muscles).

Leeds WEA branch continued to meet in Swarthmore and the Yorkshire North District offices were housed next door in number 7. The pattern that had been set up in the 1960s by Brian Thompson and the then District Secretary, Fred Sedgwick, was for the WEA to complement the practical arts activities offered by Swarthmore with serious academic classes in liberal studies and where possible to cooperate in provision, exemplified as we have seen, by collaboration on the Fresh Starts programme. The joint committee programme with Leeds University was organised through the Leeds branch in cooperation with Roger Fieldhouse, the Academic Advisor at the university. The WEA programme reflected the times with a substantial programme of politics, philosophy and history courses. A typical programme of the early 1980s offered classes on Power in Britain, Irish Culture and Politics, the Future of Work, Civil Liberties, You and the Law, Introduction to the European Community, the Rise of the Labour Party, Introduction to Ecology, Trade Union Studies, Leeds Political Economy, Nuclear Disarmament and Racism in Modern Society, as well as the feminist approaches to studies already mentioned. There were classes on Philosophy, Psychology,

Archaeology, Medieval History, Romantic Literature, Cultural Studies, Industrial Development in Leeds, Saving Historic Buildings, Contemporary Music, Cinema Studies and Ornithology as well as the distinctly New Age classes in Earth Energies by Brian Larkman and Nick Totton's Alternative Therapies. (Russell remembers finding the Earth Energies class so engrossed in discussion long after closing time, it failed to notice a greatcoat thrown over a radiator in the attic smouldering to the point of actually combusting). There was a class on the novel and film called Reading the Pictures: History Class and Culture taken by Griselda Pollock and myself which ran for a number of years. Through Janet Douglas's Local History classes that rambled through Leeds centre and suburbs on foot on balmy summer evenings, many gained inspirational insights into their city. One other particularly innovative programme was the series of Political Economy of Leeds courses initiated by Ron Wiener under the Joint Committee banner and in part funded by the Joseph Rowntree Trust, an evocation of the founders of Swarthmore. Amidst much controversy within the WEA and beyond, the classes produced three widely circulated and influential publications on the Economic, Social and Political bases of Leeds which sharply focused on the city's industrial decline and alternative strategies. Political Economy classes that met in Swarthmore included one for the very lively ecumenical Leeds Industrial Mission led by Rev. Tony Comber, later Rural Dean of Farnley, who became the Leeds WEA branch chairman.

## National Acclaim, City Scepticism

Swarthmore was well-respected nationally. It had participated in the founding of the Educational Settlements Association (ESA) in the 1920s (see Chapter 3) and still contributed to the meetings of its successor the Educational Centres Association (ECA), which offered it membership of a national movement with a well-versed forum for sharing ideas and experiences. The ECA frequently wrote letters of support in times of crisis and it was through the ECA that Alan Tuckett, Director of NIACE, first took an interest in Swarthmore's activities. He gave a ringing endorsement of its achievement in Swarthmore's 80th birthday celebration. Although warning of a harsher new climate emerging in adult education, Tuckett concluded:

> *I want to finish by celebrating something which is magic about this place... (Swarthmore members) burn with a passion and fire for learning. It's because in the end culture is made by ordinary people sharing a sense of ownership of what they are doing. And whatever else it has, Swarthmore is uniquely, I think, in Britain the place where adult learning backs its rhetoric with its practice. The amount of student control in the management of this Centre is unparalleled in Britain and I think that is important for you to know and recognise.* (Tuckett, 1989)

Without that voluntary effort and enthusiasm Swarthmore would have looked very different. The line of dedicated chairpersons and officials, like Betty Fatkin, Mark Ockleton, Roy Webber and Kay Stainsby, stretching back to its Quaker founders, those who gave up their evenings for committee work and raising funds, who kept the coffee bar running, who spotted new needs for education and harassed local authorities for no reward other than to see the Centre flourish, made it a testament to civic pride. But the sentiment was not always returned and indeed there were those on the City Council who thought that Swarthmore was too much of a good thing. They claimed it was not fulfilling its city-wide mission and muttered about the large numbers coming from more prosperous areas like Leeds 6 and Leeds 8, although in fact they were only ever around one third of the total (AR 1988–89) and seemed wilfully blind to the Centre's innovative social purpose programme. Despite its commitment to equal opportunities, it ignored the 3:1 ratio of women to men in Swarthmore's classes.

### The Financial Crisis and the Way Out

In the mid-1980s, as Russell saw it, the old officer-led LEA gave way to a politically and ideologically driven policy. Indeed the Labour group that had come to power in 1979 under George Mudie after a long period of Tory rule, was bent on radical change. It introduced for example an Industrial Committee, headed by John Battle, which drew a great deal on the Leeds Political Economy classes taught by Ron Wiener and Mike Cameron on the Joint Committee programme at Swarthmore and Anna Whyatt's courses on Co-operatives. Many of the ideas about workers' co-operatives and joint planning that had been circulating in classes were given an airing and there was for a brief period a lively spirit of innovation. However as the economic recession started to bite and the Tory government forced local councils to take deep cuts in funding, it became an opportunity for those who thought Swarthmore an arty-farty extravagance to bring it down a peg or two and in 1986 a 10% funding cut was made.

Leeds decided on reorganising its Tertiary Education (as post-school education was now called) and designated Park Lane College as the main tertiary centre in the area of Leeds that included Swarthmore. The College was required to carry out all the educational functions then shouldered by Swarthmore but concentrating on 16–19 year olds, leaving adult students with a predicament (AR 1985–86). Swarthmore was informed that the 1974 'settlement' agreed on Thompson's departure (see previous chapter) was scrapped and replaced by a new view of the Centre outlined in 'The Future Role of Swarthmore' (Appendix to 1985–86 Annual Report). The LEA would in future wish to see Swarthmore functioning as an 'out-centre' within the central Tertiary area with LEA funding allocated to work with priority groups, and with far less concentration on 'demand-led work' (by which it meant liberal studies and arts and crafts) at the Centre. This both failed to acknowledge Swarthmore's existing 'priority work' – which, as we have seen, was frequently in advance of such initiatives elsewhere in the city – and was at variance with its aims and objectives as a charity. Critically it posed a direct challenge to its autonomy.

If Leeds LEA was increasingly politically driven, it was arguably in response to an even greater ideological imperative implicit in Thatcher's 'monetarist' economic policy and licensing of greed. Equally, it may have allowed scope for a certain philistinism in the Labour approach. Swarthmore, for some, was irredeemably 'middle class' despite the fact that members were in the main far from well-heeled, frequently worked in the public sector and decidedly unloving of Mrs Thatcher's party[3]. There was no objection on Swarthmore's part to agreeing to the new LEA requirements to tackle 'priority needs' and it reminded the City of its valuable work already done. But this would depend on a continued demand-led programme of courses to fill the shortfall in income. It fell on deaf ears and a summary of the successes of the creative arts provision only confirmed the prejudices of some members.

Although the LEA funding cut was largely restored in the following years, it still fell £4,600 short of the Centre's running costs, increasing to an £8,300 deficit in 1988–89. Until 1986 Leeds had continued to honour the broad deficit funding model where a programme of courses were agreed with the LEA at the beginning of the year and normally any shortfall was made good at the end. By abandoning this convention, it compelled Swarthmore to devote even more energy to fund-raising from elsewhere. As the treasurer Mark Ockelton put it, ironically, 'such a funding formula makes priority needs education a marginal activity, rather than placing it at the centre of our attention where it belongs' (AR 1988–89: 6). Matters were not improved by the ending of the grant for Second Chance courses by the MSC and the culling of the EFS cash-crop. Swarthmore was forced to raise its fees to 85p per hour in 1989–90, meaning a 20 week course would now cost £32.

More tribulation followed in April 1990 when the LEA failed to renew the Centre's grant at all, saying that they were undertaking a major review and it would have to await the outcome. This meant that Swarthmore would have to run over half the financial year and plan a full year's programme of activity without knowing the size of its grant or whether there would be one at all. The outraged membership rose to the challenge, mass-petitioned councillors and MPs and gaining press coverage. The response from the Council was always the same, 'Wait for the outcome of the review'. When it was announced, the cut was, at almost £20,000, double that of 1985, reducing the grant to £75,000. As Russell recounts: 'There was a profound sense of injustice running through the whole centre borne of a belief that we were doing an immense amount of good work which was not being recognised, and had been treated in an outrageous and shabby manner' (Russell, personal communication 2008). The campaign culminated in a deputation to the full meeting of Leeds City Council in January 1991 led by the treasurer, Mark Ockleton, supported by over fifty students from the centre, filling the public gallery, who delivered a moving address.

Well-reported in the local papers, the campaign drew a response from the Chair of the Education Committee, Councillor Keith Burnley. Defending the LEA's position, he blamed 'Swarthmore's poor record in bringing about a radical shift in its programme in favour of the authority's priority learning groups' adding that in the light of this the £75,000 grant that had been allocated was 'very generous' (*Yorkshire Post*, 3.11.1990). Nevertheless, certain councillors had been lobbying behind the scenes and a good part of the grant was restored the following year under a covert heading. Even so, the Centre was now running an annual deficit that the City was not prepared entirely to meet, requiring an exhausting search for new sources of funding. Staff salaries and contracts were renegotiated and differential tutor fees were introduced (with LEA funded courses being paid at a higher rate than self-financing courses). Even selling the centre and relocating to another part of the city to realise some of the capital assets was seriously considered. Endless working parties, meetings, alternative proposals and mountains of paper wore down both staff and students and morale plummeted.

By September 1993 after nineteen years as Warden (and then Director when the title was changed in 1990) with yet another critical deficit, Russell resigned. Ironically, the one thing that enabled him to leave on a positive note was that as a result of the 1992 Higher and Further Education Act, he successfully applied for funding to be shifted from local to national government. Eighty per cent of the programme was then recognised for funding support through the newly created Further Education Funding Council (FEFC), leaving only the remaining 20 per cent to be wrestled from the LEA. Through an ironic twist of fate a Tory government had thrown the Centre a lifeline from a Labour authority – life under John Major had its compensations after all.

Russell had presided over a supremely creative and transformative period in Swarthmore's lifetime. It passed from a largely LEA-supported Centre to one which was to be funded largely from national government (plus a variety of other lesser sources). It had expanded and improved its buildings and facilities, nurtured the careers of many creative writers and artists, courted controversy and still remained a welcoming place for all those who just wanted to learn something new without the burden of exam-based qualifications. Another significant change was in how important it had become as an educational base for campaigning groups of all kinds from disability groups to the Campaign for Homosexual Equality. It hosted the rebirth of CND in Leeds in the early 1980s under the banner of European Nuclear Disarmament, held the crèche for the huge 'Beyond the Fragments' feminist conference in August 1980 and saw some of the first seminars of the ecological movement[4]. It was a testament to Russell's commitment to liberal education values that, even under pressure from attacks by a right wing columnist in the *Evening Post* and others, he never wavered in his commitment to open access (though he did confess on one occasion that he would be seriously worried if the National Front applied for a room).

That Swarthmore not only survived the worst of Mrs Thatcher's harrowing of the North and the ideological priorities of the Labour local authority but grew and thrived, demonstrated the strength of its voluntary movement and the vibrant sense of community it generated. It was in the best sense a collective in which responsibility for the Centre's well-being was shouldered by all. It proved how open dialogue and flexible response through the voluntary committees and widespread means of communication developed in these years, confirmed the very best in its tradition.

Staff and students outside the Swarthmore. Director Martin Russell can be seen back row left waving

## Notes

1. In fact the episode might have been described as a piece of Installation Art, before its time and, who knows, an inspiration for another of Allerton Grange's finest, at that moment taking the Foundation course at Leeds School of Art, Damien Hirst.

2. Jonathan's brother was the Centre's caretaker, Steve Phillips, who was renowned for his ability on the slide guitar, frequently performing at Swarthmore social events, often late into the night. He was an acknowledged inspiration for Mark Knopfler of Dire Straights when Knopfler was a journalist in Leeds in the 1960s. Knopfler later returned the favour by forming a country band with Phillips and another pillar of the Leeds music scene Brendon Croker (of the Five O'clock Shadows fame), calling themselves the Notting Hillbillies whose album Missing…Presumed Having a Good Time was released in 1990. Steve Phillips is now a well respected landscape painter living in Robin Hood's Bay but still plays guitar. (The Phillips brothers were in fact sons of the sculptor Harry Phillips who was himself celebrated in Mark Knopfler's song In The Gallery from the first Dire Straits album).

3. A delegation that went from the WEA Leeds branch, for example, to see Keith Joseph (then MP for NE Leeds and Minister of Education) to argue that funding cuts were harming adult education, were treated to the sage's Delphic pronouncement that 'many a mickle maks a muckle' and shown the door.

4. One infamous adventure (in which the author was centrally involved) was the Centre for Marxist Education which was based in Swarthmore for a couple of hot summers in the late 1970s. Ralph Miliband (father of David and Edward and no doubt turning in his grave) who was then Professor of Politics at Leeds University, gave regular seminars on Marx's politics, attracting up to 150 people each evening. Miliband's book Parliamentary Socialism was a scathing indictment of Labour's feeble commitment to radical reform.

## CHAPTER 7

# Educational Partnerships, Targets and Contracts, 1993–2009

The financial crisis, which was the final straw for Russell, may have encouraged the retirement of its President, Jay Blumler and its Treasurer, Mark Ockleton. Within a year its redoubtable Chair, Betty Fatkin, had gone, marking a changing of the guard and the ending of an epoch at Woodhouse Square. Swarthmore's bankers agreed to a remortgage of the property to raise the deficit amount but only on condition the Centre came up with a viable Business Plan. Swarthmore agreed to cut costs by £25,000 through axing administrative staff and crèche expenses, a time of considerable pain for all involved. Guy Farrar became the new Director in 1993 and the Chair was taken over by a long-term friend of Swarthmore, Geoff Hill, the Director of Voluntary Action Leeds, with whom the Centre had worked on a number of joint volunteering projects. Hill was used to working creatively with the restrictions of prioritised funding and helped reorientate Swarthmore towards the new exigencies. As a result over the next few years, a leaner staff and restructured executive led Swarthmore into the brave new world of 'targets'.

One of Russell's last acts as Director (as we saw in the previous chapter) had been successfully to apply to the newly created FEFC for funding, which meant that most courses would now be funded from national government rather than local sources. However, students would be required to submit to accreditation. While this went against the grain for many, it appeared to be the only way to regain some independence and as a result the Open College Network (OCN) became the principal agent for accreditation. Farrar was an enthusiast for accreditation, holding, not without reason, that it offered adults who had missed out on earlier educational chances the opportunity to gain qualifications. He made it into a successful enterprise and many students benefited from the qualifications they achieved. Thus Swarthmore would now have to respond to targets set by the FEFC, whose inspectors would in due course visit the Centre to review progress. Future funding would depend on how well targets were met. With its main funding now drawn from national sources, Swarthmore could more comfortably work with Leeds City Council to meet the needs of its priority student groups. Needless to say, this affected recruitment of students. Higher fees reduced enrolment on the self-funded courses (those not supported by either Leeds LEA or the FEFC) mainly in the Arts and Crafts and other non-accredited liberal studies, by about 300. But a corresponding rise in numbers on accredited courses of 200 meant the overall drop was only around 100. Since the late 1960s Swarthmore's overall student recruitment had hovered around 2,000 annually, dropping immediately when a hike in fees was imposed but gradually rising again thereafter. Enrolment was now down to about 1,500 initially but over the year another 400 were added.

New Swarthmore Director Guy Farrar, right, is welcomed by Martin Russell the retiring Director

Swarthmore's bid to the FEFC had been well-supported by Park Lane College, with whom it had built up a good working relationship over the previous decade. In 1995-96 its first inspection by the FEFC was positive and its funding was increased by 20% to £98,000. Leeds appeared to recognise Swarthmore's contribution by raising its funding by 50% to £30,000 (AR 1994-95). Added together this represented a little over half of all income to the Centre. Remarkably, fees raised from self-funding courses were almost the same as the FEFC funding at around £98,500, the remainder coming from grants and donations from other sources such as NIACE, Thackrays, the Reckitt Foundation, YHA and the Friends. By 1995 total income was around £280,000 and represented a balancing of the books at last. The management structure was refined by merging the Executive and Council and new committees formed with, for the first time, a Financial Committee responsible for overall financial management (previously Swarthmore Executive was the financial arm of Council and responsible for financial management). Equal Opportunities were now the responsibility of the Personnel and Employment Committee and a Publicity and Promotion Committee developed a new and increasingly targeted approach to publicity. A part time Assistant Director was appointed and to cope with the burgeoning bureaucracy caused by the new modes of funding and accreditation, more part-time administrators were recruited.

So with the newly negotiated mortgage from the bank and more secured funding, the crisis was lessening. Leeds City Council now funded a revised version of the Fresh Starts course with Jane Daguerre as coordinator and targeted more specifically at disadvantaged groups (through its recently created Community Benefits and Rights F.E. Client Unit). However, the emphasis now was on employability, careers guidance and practical skills with taster courses in the arts, rather than the original intensive courses in liberal studies that could lead on to Further or Higher Education.

### Multiple Provision

Various new 'partnership' arrangements were set up. Yorkshire Arts, a long standing supporter, funded a new Arts development post, filled by Edyn Culverwell (who left only in Summer 2008 to take up a post at Mind the Gap theatre company in Bradford). Andy Berisford, a well-liked tutor in the

Arts, had done some development work in the 90s. Courses for people with disabilities (with PATH) became a major day-time feature, offering tasters in the practical arts, music, singing and dance. With VAL the Centre offered short courses to develop skills such as Report Writing, Promotional writing, Minute Taking and Public Speaking for active involvement in local communities and cultural groups. Volunteering opportunities grew and an initial training course in working with disabled people was offered. So a new pattern began to emerge where targeting through partnerships took a much greater role in the profile of the Centre, especially during the day.

Accredited courses increased substantially. Around eight GCSE courses were offered in a range of subjects: Social Policy, English Language, Art and Design, Mathematics (taught by Marjorie Hall a long-time stalwart of the WEA and Swarthmore), Health Studies, Modern Greek, Law and General Studies, in a small but popular programme. Counselling courses led by Hazel Hobbs continued to grow in number and scope ranging from introductory classes to the RSA Certificate in Counselling Skills and now became associated with Personal Development classes, over a dozen courses annually. An addition to the programme was the revival of Communication Skills for the British Sign Language Certificate and Makaton (a vocabulary for communicating with people lacking verbal skills). Health Issues became a new enlarged element in the programme offering accredited courses by St Johns Ambulance and GCSE in Health Studies. But New Age approaches like Aromatherapy, Herbal Medicine and Hypnotherapy, Meditation and Reflexology continued to be popular as did classes in Alexander Technique. Computing provision from Introductory to RSA Certification, rose to around 12 courses annually, along with a suite of new technology.

The languages programme was, for the moment, still a significant element of the Centre, offering around 25 courses in French, German, Italian, Spanish, Greek, Japanese, Chinese and Urdu at levels 1–3, which included voluntary accreditation (through the OCN) in a relaxed atmosphere. However, before long demand fell sharply, partly because of similar courses offered at Park Lane, complete with a language learning suite at competitive rates but because of a more general decline in language learning across the country. (Over 500,000 part time language students were lost from colleges and other centres since 2000 as the result of a directive from the LSC which deemed this provision to be low priority). Thus after nearly 90 years of more or less continuous provision, which in the inter-war years had promoted a lively spirit of internationalism, languages dropped from the programme. A small programme, however, may be offered in 2009.

The Arts and Crafts which had in many ways come to command Swarthmore's identity in the post-war years, as we have seen, maintained their presence with around 35 courses being offered in an even wider range of practices such as: Painting, Pottery, Sculpture, Jewellery, Printmaking, Etching, Photography, Weaving, Calligraphy, Embroidery, Batik, Chinese Brushstroke and even, for some years, Hat Making. Pam Rex and Molly Lord continued to inspire new students through Drawing, Portraiture and Pottery classes as did Diane Barnes, Jo Aris, and David Collins. Roger Barnes taught his unique jewellery crafts, while Diane Cross continued with original Pottery classes along with Stan Stemp and the remarkable Iranian artist Karen Babayan taught Life Drawing, while newer tutors included Simon Dobbs. A growing number of classes now offered the OCN and GCSE qualifications, necessary for FEFC funding. The Creative Writing and Literature programme led by Jean Stevens expanded into around nine courses a year and diversified into Fiction writing, Playwriting, Poetry, writing for Children and a course exploring the work of Black Women Writers.

Dance, Movement and Keep Fit organised by Liz Normaschild offered mixed ability courses which included Ballroom Dancing, Contemporary Dance, and Circle Dancing. For the first time courses were offered for children and parents and toddlers. Sadly, Liz died in the late 1990s and was much missed. Yoga and T'ai Chi remained popular and courses for Self Defence for Women, including Karate, continued a theme begun in the late 1970s. Another of the arts that had become well-established since that time was music and around six courses were offered in Guitar, Folk Fiddle, Tin Whistle and singing in a choir. The increasing popularity of Family History and Gardening may have reflected a more subdued time in Swarthmore's affairs, with students more concerned to explore where they came from or dig their own plot, which concluded a diverse and popular programme of courses.

Folk Music Workshop, 2005

The partnership with the WEA Leeds branch and Philip Ralph, the Tutor Organiser, was still important to Swarthmore and its liberal studies programme was able to complement the Centre's arts and crafts provision but it was considerably reduced. The WEA offered courses in Art and Architecture, World Cinema (though no longer with its pioneer Les Rayner who had died), Art History, Indian Civilization, Philosophy, York Medieval History and Creative Writing. The only science course was in the Natural History of the Yorkshire Dales and the only social science class was an introduction to Psychology. Women's studies were still popular and included a course on women's health, the representation of women in literature and assertiveness training. Around seven courses were provided jointly with Leeds University and were accredited by them, the old Joint Committee arrangement having lapsed because of the requirement of the 1992 FE and HE Act for university continuing education courses to be 'mainstreamed' and accredited (leading to an HE qualification). However a number of courses seemed to overlap those on Swarthmore's mainstream programme, including creative writing, drama and music workshops, although they often reflected alternative approaches to the subject. By 2001 WEA courses were no longer included in the brochure and it was clear that Swarthmore's life-long relationship with the WEA Leeds branch was faltering.

The WEA as a national organisation was suffering its own funding problems and the rigours of accreditation, which it too had long resisted. With parking around Swarthmore in the evening becoming increasingly difficult, the Leeds branch decided to concentrate on its extended programme around the city, instead.

In 1998, after a very hectic five years in which Swarthmore was successfully reorientated to the new priorities, Guy Farrar left to work for the OCN and Ann Walker was appointed Director in his place, the first woman to fill the leading role at the Centre. Although the new direction was consolidated, finances were still not secure and a cumulative deficit had built up once more, resulting in £19,000 deficit in 1998 (AR, 1999–2000). This was addressed by another recovery plan and a further management restructuring. As the times demanded, the annual reports became even more dominated by statistics, in a cascade of bullet-pointed facts and figures, confirming that targets had been met. For the first time information about the ethnic makeup of its students was given, showing at least 10% reported themselves as Black or Asian, which almost exactly mirrored the Leeds census (2001) proportion, and 16% were 'disabled' (Leeds, 2002). The proportion of women members had increased from around two thirds in the 1960s to 75% and the average age had risen somewhat, although just over a half were under 40. Partnership arrangements with local or national agencies were becoming more important. The latest of these was with Leeds Training and Enterprise Council for a three year programme of courses for parents and carers to take an interest in children's learning, called the 'I Too Community Education Project'. A related programme called Twilight 2000 for after hours family learning for 'families on means tested benefits' received £25,000 from the Millennium Festival Fund and was launched by Hilary Benn MP. By the millennium Swarthmore's income had risen to £430,000 and a healthy surplus of £45,000 (equivalent to its whole budget in 1960) had been achieved.

Swarthmore's governing profile was changing. Irene Heron, a Creative Writing tutor, took over the Chair and Martin Wainwright succeeded Jay Blumler as President. The son of the former Liberal MP for the Colne Valley, Richard Wainwright, and the brother of the campaigning socialist journalist, Hilary, whose organ *Red Pepper* continues to 'spice up' the Left, Martin Wainwright is well known for his witty and insightful commentaries on 'Northern life' in the *Guardian*. The relationship with Leeds City Council had improved markedly and in 1999 Swarthmore's 90th birthday celebrations, were attended by former leader of the council, George Mudie MP.

## Lifelong Learning or Adult Education?

In the new language of 'Lifelong learning' that had accompanied New Labour's educational policy, the Centre now described its 'core programme' as provision for the 'excluded' and educational courses had become subtly retitled as 'learning activities'. This reflected a shift from teaching-centred 'education' to student-centred 'learning' and a concern for the perspective of the students or 'learners' as they were now known, rather than the providing institution – 'learning styles' replaced 'teaching modes' as the dominant discourse. In some sense this shift of emphasis was something adult educators had been pursuing since the 1970s when UNESCO first promoted *education permanente* – although in truth it went back to Basil Yeaxlee in the 1920s (Yeaxlee, 1929). But it could be said that this was always Swarthmore's style of provision and the language had only now caught up with the practice (one particularly regrettable piece of the new style vocabulary, however, was that courses were not so much 'taught' as 'delivered', like the mail). However, the programme at Swarthmore in some ways had gone back one stage further than that of its founders – who always assumed a substantial literacy among its working class students – to the Quaker (and especially Rowntree) 'deficit education' classes of the mid-19th century (see Chapter One). 'Targeting' meant that once again it was the most deprived students at whom core courses were aimed – and a sad commentary on the failure of the welfare state to eliminate poverty and severe social deprivation over the intervening century and a half. Moreover, Swarthmore's founders believed they were educating a working class élite to lead the labour movement into the new era of democracy and social justice through their own abilities, rather than the charity of their employers. Education was to provide the tools for a new political order based on fellowship and equality and a rational belief that, if only people understood more about themselves and the world they lived in through applied study, social problems could be solved. By the millennium, however, 'targeting' had abandoned any such utopian aims and usually meant preparing people from deprived backgrounds for the labour market, cultivating confidence in their own abilities and attempting to equip them with skills to make a living.

Swarthmore, of course, took this on board and created a series of partnerships with the local authority and other agencies. The 2000-2001 Annual Report listed relationships and contracted work with over 20 agencies and providers. It was now embedded in an extensive national and local network specialising in these policies. With the DES Neighbourhood Support Fund it set up a 'Plus One' project for teenage parents; with UK Online it became a centre offering access to computer technology; with Creative Partnerships in Education (CAPE UK) it had a project with young people that included drama, video production and IT. Meanwhile Twilight 2000 and 'I Too' with Chris Hoy as the new Community Education Worker carried on a further year. Swarthmore was more involved with local community initiatives like Little Woodhouse Community Association and Rosebank Millenium Green Trust. Another significant change was that this expansion of activity relied much less on members' voluntarism and, consequently, Swarthmore's 'core staff' had now risen to 24 (not all full-time). The staff role-call now included: the Director, Finance/Services Manager, Arts Manager, Counselling and Personal Development Manager, Learning Support Manager, ICT Manager, Information Services Manager, Centre Administrators, Learning Support Assistant, 3 Reception staff, 5 caretakers, 3 coffee bar staff, 2 childcare staff and 2 technicians. The Centre was now a substantial employer and, though still a registered charity, increasingly resembled a small to medium sized business (SME) with an income (£480,000) to match and a payroll of £332,000.
Not surprisingly, in 2003 Swarthmore took the precaution of registering as limited company to take account of its burgeoning liabilities.

In 2002 Ann Walker, to the Centre's great regret, moved next door to become District Secretary of the WEA, Yorkshire District following Sam Herman's retirement and in August Malcolm Walters was appointed Director. Walters came from a substantial background in Community Education in Leeds and the West Riding and knew the ropes from the local authority angle. Other contextual changes affected Swarthmore. For some years, because of perceived failure, education in Leeds had been taken out of local control by the

Jewellery workshop, 2005

government and in 2001 it had passed into the hands of a not-for-profit company called Education Leeds, describing itself as: 'a unique partnership between Leeds City Council and Capita and operated under a direction from the Secretary of State for Education and Skills'. Though sceptically viewed by many, this was good news for the Centre, at least: Leeds City Council decided to raise its annual grant to £89,000, increasing the hourly rate on which it was calculated for the first time since 1993.

In yet another flush of political acronymity the FEFC was replaced by the LSC (Learning and Skills Council) and Swarthmore's grant was raised by 5% to £250,000, roughly maintaining the balance of local/national funding set up since 1993 but now providing nearly two thirds of the Centre's income (from just under one half previously). The remarkable rise in income continued until 2005 when it reached its peak at almost £955,000 (AR 2006-2007: 12). This was the most Swarthmore ever accrued in a twelve month period and it's worth for a moment looking at the sources. Significantly, fees (including membership fees) rose only to £113,000 or 12% of the total, probably the *lowest* proportion it had ever been (compare with 1994 when fees produced almost the same amount and represented 45% of the total). Income from 'Educational Contracts', as the mainstream funding from Leeds CC, LSC and other contract funding, reached £666,000 or nearly 70% of all income. Rents accounted for £72,000 (7.5%) and coffee bar receipts £65,000 (7%) - their combined total generating more than fees.

Together with registering as a limited liability company, this represented what, in the context of Higher Education funding after WW2, Eric Ashby had called a 'climacteric'. Swarthmore was now very much an educational *enterprise*, and although still wholly independent in spirit, received the overwhelming bulk of its income from contracted provision rather than traditional sources. This trend had of course been developing over the previous two decades, when serious cuts in LEA funding forced it to look elsewhere. But, put another way, since 1993-94 the Centre's income had practically quadrupled to its 2005 figure (from £247,000 to £955,000). Staffing and consequently wages and salaries reflected this change. It couldn't last, could it? Well, pressure from the LSC enforced a rise of 5% in fees the following year - with the usual negative effect on recruitment to non-funded classes. And over the next two years contract funding fell to £523,000 (-21%) while fee income rose by only £17,000 (+15%). By 2007 the Centre's total income had fallen to £823,000, an overall drop of 14% from the 2005 peak.

But, as in every crisis, Swarthmore saw it as an opportunity for renewal and reflection. John Arnison took over as Chair from Freda Matthews, who mounted a fascinating exhibition of local history and Travellers at the Centre. Sadly, Pam Rex's death was announced, 'a great inspiration to generations of students' and a great loss to all who knew her (AR 2006-07). It was regretted too, that Walters, who had initiated much of the Centenary proposals, could not see them through to fruition and announced his intention to retire at the end of the year (2007). Maggi Butterworth was appointed Director in the New Year.

## Users and Volunteers

Had the composition of the Centre noticeably changed? In some ways things looked very different. Much more of the day time provision was now reserved for targeted groups while what were now called 'leisure class' students were largely found in the evening. Overall student numbers had remained relatively constant at around 2000 but declined in 2006-07 to 1808 (although actual enrolments were 2836, due presumably to students enrolling on more than one course) of whom over a half were in free or concessionary places. The average age had crept up somewhat with now a slight majority over 40 years, while the proportion of women to men lowered a little to 71% and disability accounted for 18% of students (AR 2006-07: 4). Around 29% lived locally to the city centre, the biggest single group (16%) coming from Leeds 6 as always.

But there had always been special groups of one kind or another using the Centre, from the Jewish refugees of the inter-war years, the Army during WW2, the Trade Union day release students and Marxists of the 1970s, the unemployed and Foreign Language students of the 1980s, as well as the odd colourful Bohemian gatherings, jazz, folk and punk musicians, overflows from Leeds FE Colleges and assorted vagrants. Swarthmore was just that kind of place. The buildings were constantly being refurbished for project work and resources like those for the crèche and playgroup and computing. The roof always needed repairing and fund-raising drives would haul the money in. In 2005 a Community Capital Grant was secured to renovate rooms in No. 2 which had previously been let out to the Pavilion feminist photography Gallery. For the first time, the following year, Swarthmore managed to get a capital allocation grant from the LSC of £26,500 which was used for building repairs and replacing computers.

By 2005 the programme brochure returned to its normal A5 size from the colourful (but almost unreadable) A4 size of the previous years and the structure of provision remained relatively constant, but shifts were taking place. Return to Learn taster classes were replaced by a programme of over 20 Skills for Life classes concentrating on the 3Rs, Basic Home maintenance, Sign Language, Introduction to Computing and Healthy Living. Counselling and Personal Development classes grew in number and a new Advanced Certificate was introduced. Computing expanded substantially with a programme of 11 workshops leading to CLAIT qualifications at various levels and some non-accredited courses in, for example, Website Creation.

The Arts programme maintained its size partly through increased OCN accreditation (which meant courses were supported by grant aid from the LSC). The First Step Arts Courses, supported by Leeds CC, aimed at unemployed and 'new learners' (first-time students) were intended as an introduction to the arts and crafts to gain confidence and possibly progress to accredited levels. For those paying full fees, courses now cost on average £138 for 20 weeks with extra charges for materials. The well-established courses in painting, drawing, jewellery pottery and sculpture were (in the traditional spirit of response to demand) complemented by new additions including puppetry, frame making, quilting, sewing and stained glass making, some of which were aimed at children and first timers. Music, Dance and Drama maintained a high profile of around ten courses annually and now included African Drumming and Salsa in response to the growing interest in World Music and Afro-Cuban culture. The People's Choir was also complemented by the disarmingly 'out' Gay Abandon choir. Creative Writing grew back to around four classes, one of which was accredited by the OCN and another supported by First Step, which now included Screen

Writing. A new category in the programme was Healthy Living which included over 20 courses in Aromatherapy, Hypnotherapy, Massage, several kinds of Yoga, and T'ai Chi but now Pilates, Gentle Exercise and '5 Rhythms'.

While the 'traditional' self-funded programme maintained its profile, the targeted programme developed what were now called Community Learning Projects. These included a course run at Careers Leeds called New Directions for carers trying to create new lives for themselves. Another continuing partner was Education Leeds Alternative Programme (another department of Leeds CC) which contracted with Swarthmore to introduce disaffected young people to an alternative educational experience to schooling, giving them taster sessions in the arts and crafts and computing, leading to qualifications. A new field of work was with refugees and asylum seekers in partnership with People in Action. Around 50 people benefited from accredited courses in literacy, numeracy, ICT and the OCN qualification in working with disabled people. ESOL courses were run again at Swarthmore as well as at Rosebank Primary School.

A significant renewal of links to the movement that had founded Swarthmore nearly a century previously came with the Centre's new association with Airton Meeting House, run by the Quakers, near Malham. A number of sessions were held here during the year including a Hand Drumming course. A previous resident of Swarthmore's premises, who had been a significant art patron in the nineteenth century, was Ellen Heaton. Council decided an annual memorial lecture in her name should be given. The first of these memorial lectures was given by Brett Harrison on Holocaust Survivors in Yorkshire, many of whom found a welcome at Swarthmore on arrival in Leeds. In the second, given by the celebrated feminist historian, Jill Liddington, the Leeds suffragette, Leonora Cohen, was honoured. Cohen's militant activities in Leeds, campaigning for votes for women coincided with Swarthmore's early days and shared in the crusading atmosphere (Liddington, 2006).

### Swarthmore's Century

So as the Centenary approached Swarthmore appeared yet again to have transformed itself in order to stay in business, because indeed that was what it was forced to become. The very proliferation of funding agencies is matched only by the Centre's nimble ability to offer a 'contracted' service to each. To take the example of Leeds City Council: for at least three quarters of its existence the Centre's primary relationship was with what was then called the Local Education Authority (LEA) which gradually developed its grant-aid, until it was the major funder. Some years after this relationship was put under pressure by national funding restrictions and a broader failure in policy, the LEA was replaced by a government appointed quango. By this time Swarthmore had successfully switched most of its funding to the FEFC and then the LSC, as we have seen. Leeds City Council's funding was then disbursed through various sub-divisions and contractual relations for targeted provision were agreed. Although at times it must have been near impossible to keep up with the chameleon changes in top-labelling, these now included the Adult and Community Education section of Jobs and Skills which funded First Step and Personal and Community Development classes, and Education Leeds Alternative Programme which catered for disaffected 14-16 year olds, a very challenging group. Swarthmore's current major funder, the LSC, as we have seen, emerged from the dissolution of the FEFC, itself a creation of the 1992 FE and HE Act. Without any noticeable philosophical debate about the distinction between education and training, education and 'skills' became increasingly interwoven so that even the Ministry of Education gradually incorporated the title, changing itself into the Department for Education and Skills (DfES). That lasted only a few years and currently, renamed as the Department for Children, Schools and Families (DCFS), it has dropped 'education', and even 'skills', from its title altogether. Yet another derivative of government, the Skills Fund, finances work, such as that with Calderdale College, to run 'low level accredited courses in Skills for Life and ICT' (AR 2006-07), while Igen (West Yorkshire Careers) funds educational advice sessions for students. The government's policy of Lifelong Learning was silently replaced by the 'Skills Agenda' and funding tied even more closely to employment needs.

Ever resourceful, Swarthmore was forced to raise income from other sources. Rents from the property have climbed steadily to nearly £80,000 annually, the Hall being currently let out during the day to Park Lane College. Less palatably, the wage bill has had to be reduced and has fallen by 11% from its 2005 high of £578,000. What has long since ceased to be a major source of funding, are donations from charitable (often Quaker) organisations while fees, which until the early-1990s accounted for almost a half of the total income, now contribute around 16% (although in some respects funding from Leeds and elsewhere conceals a hidden fee element).

So far this chapter has (perhaps unavoidably) centred on statistical and administrative themes and has ignored the members who are the life blood of Swarthmore. What was it like to be part of the student democracy during these years? For over 40 years Kay Stainsby was a very engaged member of the Centre and many aspects of her story are typical. They trace the routes from student to tutor, Council member and for a while part time Assistant Director. Attracted by the friendly atmosphere of the Centre, Kay joined an Art class when her youngest child first attended Primary School in 1968. She shortly became a class representative and then joined the House Committee, which amongst other things ran the coffee bar. Kay frequently served behind the bar, helped organise the volunteer staff and looked after the accounts. She was active in the Preschool Playgroups Association, then instrumental in raising the social issue of childcare, and suggested Swarthmore ran its own playgroup for parents attending classes. Council adopted the plan and facilities continue until this day. Kay was elected to Council and has served on it ever since with a stint on the Programme Planning Committee and as a voluntary tutor for the Literacy programme. She tutored a weekly study group in Wildflower Studies looking at identification, geography and ecological elements. On Council she supported the introduction of the path-breaking Fresh Start programme, counselling courses and a limited number of examination courses but above all providing activities for the educationally deprived and closer contacts with local communities. In latter years, the complexities of funding have tested her severely – which she puts down to old age – but her dedication clearly demonstrates the difference that can be made by an active voluntary movement in adult education. As Kay is the first to acknowledge, she gained a great deal in return from Swarthmore which has played a big part in her life. The current Chair of Council, John Arnison, has been instrumental in renewing links with the Friends, particularly in relation to advancing social inclusion. He has reintroduced a Quaker meeting for worship on the first Wednesday of the month at Swarthmore and has started a homeless memorial service – 'very cathartic for all the people involved'. John intends to walk from Leeds to London in 2009 for the 'Raise the roof appeal'.

## Swarthmore's Next Century

How is Swarthmore shaping up for its next century? Over the last three decades it has made a remarkable effort to transform itself from a liberal arts-based adult education centre to incorporate a largely day-time resource for the educationally deprived. While the ethos of the liberal arts centre is successfully maintained through a full cost 'leisure' programme in the Arts and Crafts in the evenings, funding priorities are directed at the day-time courses.

Under the globalised pressure of providing for a constantly 'upskilled' and qualified work-force, national policy towards post-compulsory education has changed substantially in recent years. The administration of the whole of the Further, Adult and Higher Education sector has been devolved by the government to a new ministry, the Department for Innovation, Universities and Skills (DIUS). Sadly, the specific vocation of Adult Education has tended to get lost in the process and it is increasingly treated as a subsidiary arm of FE, rather than as a sector in its own right. Seeing numbers in adult education declining alarmingly (around 1.4 million) and funding disappearing, Alan Tuckett at NIACE has with increasing urgency raised the problem with ministers. In 2008, the DIUS sent out a 'Consultation' document about the future of Informal Adult Learning and NIACE's response made clear its own concerns:

> *However the consultation comes after a period of rapid restructuring of public support for adult learning, an overall drop in participation in learning adults choose for themselves, and in particular a reduction of provision in the areas of first steps learning and 'other further education'. To maximise public confidence and secure the best benefit from this positive re-framing, NIACE believes Government should seek to secure change that will leave learners in structured, and self-directed informal learning feeling better supported.* (NIACE, 2008)

Swarthmore's own written response to the consultation reflected these concerns and added a few of its own, while displaying its hopes for the future (Swarthmore, 2008). In summary, Swarthmore made clear that it attracts a wide social mix of people and for a significant number the Centre is 'a life line and the highlight of their week'. Many people are referred onto courses by different agencies and around 60% of current learners have a long term health problem, often with learning difficulties. Importantly, many have started their learning process through one of the First Steps courses in the Arts, then moving on to improve their Maths or English or to Level 2 and 3 courses in Arts and Crafts. Swarthmore has not only a substantial professional staff to deal with the specific needs of educationally deprived students but is crucially supported by many volunteers for whom the Centre's work is a valuable use of their time and energy.

Target driven qualifications, the response continues, are not always the best way of improving learning and Swarthmore pleads for greater flexibility. Similarly, the constant hike in fees is driving away low-earners and while 'We still believe that those who can afford to pay for adult learning should do [...] there should be fully funded provision for those who are at risk of social exclusion and living in poverty' (Swarthmore 2008). Like other providers, Swarthmore has taken its share in cuts to adult education budgets over the last few years and made many courses, like the Level Four Diploma in Therapeutic Counselling, full cost. But students are struggling and the infrastructure itself is suffering badly. More cuts could mean the adult education service disappearing entirely despite the sacrifices it has made:

> *We moved on a long time ago from the 70s and have changed from those liberal non voc days to a model that grew in the 90s. We really were victims of our own success by widening participation and entrenching the belief in lifelong learning.* (Ibid)

But it has retained the traditional values that have distinguished the best sort of liberal adult education: 'We put our learners at the heart of everything we do. Swarthmore encourages learners to negotiate the content of their informal learning and ensure that their learning objectives are relevant and fulfilling'.

**The conclusion offers a heartfelt plea to the government:**

> *We are in danger of creating an under-class with current Government policy of funding across the FE sector and the narrow view that skills training in favour of a second or third chance to an education brings. Learning should be an integral part of life from childhood to old age in an enlightened, tolerant and resourceful society and should be accessible regardless of age, income and personal circumstances. Adult learning is not just about skills acquisition, it enriches the lives of families and communities...Do we have to wait until there are riots on the street again for funding to be secured?* (Ibid)

Against the odds, Swarthmore has maintained a programme of liberal arts education combined with prioritised work with the educationally deprived, having had to wrench itself in new directions to do so. It has changed shape in many ways over its century, while retaining its core values: from a home for educating Quaker Adult School leaders for what it hoped was the new working-class democracy, to an internationalist centre for refugees between the wars, to a khaki-clad language school during World War Two, to a centre for understanding social reconstruction after war, to a literary and philosophical refuge in the 1950s, to an avant-garde Arts Centre in the 1960s, a centre for community politics, social debate and the arts in the '70s and '80s, and lastly in the '90s and 2000s a refocusing on the educationally neglected, while maintaining its liberal arts base. All the while, through its membership and voluntary workers it has felt like a home rather than an institution; it is an essential part of the fabric of civic life in Leeds, without which Leeds would be much the poorer. It offers a shining model for the future health of any city that takes the educational welfare of its citizens seriously.

EDUCATIONAL PARTNERSHIPS, TARGETS AND CONTRACTS, 1993-2009

The five most recent Wardens at the Swarthmore Centenary Civic Reception at Leeds Civic Hall, 16 February 2009. Left to right: Martin Russell, Guy Farrar, Ann Walker, Malcolm Walters and Maggi Butterworth.

**APPENDIX 1**     **Wardens and Directors 1909-2009**

| | |
|---|---|
| **Gerald Kenway Hibbert** | Warden 1909-1919 |
| **Maurice Rowntree** | Lecturer and Sub-Warden 1909-1917 |
| **Richard Swain** | Assistant Warden 1917-1919 |
| **T. Edmund Harvey** | Warden: 1920-21 |
| **Charles E. Hodgson** | Warden: 1921-27 (Sub-Warden: 1920) |
| **Wilfrid Allott** | Warden: 1927-42 |
| **Stanley Thompson** | Warden (acting): 1942-43 |
| **Desmond Neill** | Warden: 1943-46 |
| **Maurice Hughes** | Warden: 1946-49 |
| **Geoffrey Hines** | Warden: 1949-59 |
| **Brian Stapleton** | Warden: 1959-64 |
| **Brian Thompson** | Warden: 1964-73 |
| **Paul Roche** | Warden (acting): 1973-74 |
| **Martin Russell** | Warden: 1974-90; Director: 1990-93 |
| **Guy Farrar** | Director: 1993-98 |
| **Ann Walker** | Director: 1998-2002 |
| **Malcolm Walters** | Director: 2002-2008 |
| **Maggi Butterworth** | Director: 2008 continuing |

# Swarthmore Annual Income

**APPENDIX 2**

(in pounds sterling)

| Year | Income |
|---|---|
| 1910 | 900 |
| 1911 | 935 |
| 1914 | 987 |
| 1916 | 905 |
| 1920 | 887 |
| 1938 | 1,097 |
| 1945 | 1,769 |
| 1956 | 3,317 |
| 1962 | 9,600 |
| 1967 | 14,000 |
| 1973 | 27,000 |
| 1976 | 24,000 |
| 1985 | 130,000 |
| 1989 | 176,000 |
| 1995 | 280,000 |
| 2001 | 480,000 |
| 2005 | 955,000 |
| 2007 | 823,000 |

# References

Addams, Jane (1910) *Twenty Years at Hull House*, New York: Macmillan. Reprinted at www.infed.org/archives/e-texts/addams18.htm, accessed 15 Oct 2008.

Allaway, A. J. (1961) *The educational centres movement: a comprehensive survey*. London: National Institute of Adult Education.

Allott, Wilfred (1949) 'Growth and Development', Swarthmore 40th Annual Report.

Anon (probably Allott) *A Leeds Experiment in Adult Education 1909-1930*. Swarthmore, 21st Annual Report.

Bennett, Gay and Hall, Marjorie (1999) Notes for History of Swarthmore (unpublished) Swarthmore Archives.

Beresford, Maurice (1989) Notes for a lecture on Sir Michael Sadler, delivered in the University of Leeds on 28 April 1989, Brotherton Library Special Collections, University of Leeds.

Briggs, Asa and Macartney, Anne (1984) *Toynbee Hall The First Hundred Years*. London: Routledge Keegan Paul.

Croft, Linda (2002) *This is the District, we are the People a history of the WEA in Yorkshire*. Leeds: WEA Yorkshire North District

Dover Wilson, John (1928) Adult Education in Yorkshire, *Journal of Adult Education*, Vol. III, October 1928.

Dover Wilson, John (1969) *Milestones on the Dover Road*. London: Faber and Faber.

Fieldhouse, Roger (1986) *Adult Education and the Cold War*. Leeds: Leeds Studies in Adult Education.

Fieldhouse, Roger with associates (1996) *A history of modern British adult education*. Leicester: NIACE.

Freeman, Mark (2004) *The Joseph Rowntree Charitable Trust, A Study in Quaker Philanthropy and Adult Education 1904-1954.* York: Sessions of York.

Freeman, Mark (2008) *Quaker Extension c.1905–1930: The Yorkshire 1905 Committee.* York, University of York, Borthwick Paper, No.112.

Gillman, John Frederick (1916) *The Workers and Education a record of some present day experiments.* London: George Allen & Unwin

Great Britain. Ministry of Reconstruction. Adult Education Committee. (1980) *The 1919 Report / the final and interim reports of the Adult Education Committee of the Ministry of Reconstruction.* Reprinted with introductory essays by Harold Wiltshire ... [et al.]. Nottingham: Department of Adult Education, University of Nottingham.

Hanna, Ian, (1964) *A socio-psychological survey of the student membership of adult education classes in Leeds and changes in the adult education student population since 1945* unpublished Leeds, Thesis (M.A.), (Department of Adult Education and Psychology), University of Leeds.

Hannam, June (1989) *Isabella Ford.* Oxford: Basil Blackwell.

Harrison, John (1961) *Learning and Living 1790–1960.* London: Routledge and Kegan Paul.

Harvey, T. Edmund (1949) 'Experiment in Adult Education', Swarthmore 40th Annual Report.

Hibbert, Gerald Kenway (1949) article in Swarthmore 40th Annual Report.

Hibbert, Gerald Kenway (1911) *Swarthmore and St Mary's: An Expression of Modern Quakerism.* no publication details (Leeds City Reference Library).

Hughes, Maurice W. (1949) 'Swarthmore 1943–49' article in Swarthmore 40th Annual Report.

Jepson, N. A. (1973) *The Beginnings of English University Adult Education – Policy and Problems.* London: Michael Joseph.

Kennedy, Thomas C. (2001) *British Quakerism 1860–1920: the transformation of a religious community.* Oxford: Oxford University Press.

Leeds Census (2002) (http://www.leeds.gov.uk/files/Internet2007/2006/week13/inter__868a20ca-6e3c-4039-8f06-61345391b5aa_d59ab249-4827-476a-bf5a-ec26e12407c4.pdf.)

Liddington, Jill (2006) *Rebel Girls their fight for the vote*. London: Virago.

Ludlum, Len (ed) (1959) *Jubilee magazine*. Leeds: Swarthmore Educational Centre,

Milne, Seamus (2004) *The Enemy Within MI5 Maxwell and the Scargill Affair*. London: Verso.

Sadleir, Michael (1949) *Michael Ernest Sadler a Memoir by his Son*. London: Constable.

Stapleton, G. B. (1964) 'Cooperation, a View from the Centre' in *Adult Education* Vol xxxvii, No 1 May, 1964: 14-17.

Stapleton, Mike (2006) Obituary of Brian Stapleton, *Guardian* 3/3/2006.

Steele, Tom (1987) 'Class Consciousness to Cultural Studies, the WEA in Yorkshire, *Studies in the Education of Adults*, Vol. 19, No. 2, 1987: 109-126.

Steele, Tom (1990) *Alfred Orage and the Leeds Arts Club 1903-1923*. Basingstoke, Scolar Press.

Steele, Tom (1997) *The Emergence of Cultural Studies 1945-65 Cultural Politics, Adult Education and the English Question*. London: Lawrence and Wishart,

Steele, Tom (2007) *Knowledge is Power! The Rise and Fall of European Popular Education Movements, 1848-1939*. Frankfurt: Peter Lang.

Swindells, Julia (1995) Are we not more than half the nation? Women and the 'Radical Tradition' of Adult Education, 1867-1919, in (eds) Marjorie Mayo and Marjorie and Jane Thompson, *Adult Learning Critical Intelligence*. Leicester: NIACE.

Tuckett, Alan (1989) 'A Moment in the Sun', a lecture to commemorate the 80th anniversary of Swarthmore, in Swarthmore 80th Annual Report.

Woodhouse, Tom (1996) *Nourishing the Liberty Tree Liberals and Labour in Leeds 1880-1890*. Keele: Keele University Press.

Yeaxlee, Basil A. (1929) *Lifelong education: a sketch of the range and significance of the adult education movement*. London: Cassell and Co.